HOW TO TALK TO ANYBODY WITH CONFIDENCE

Master the Art of Conversation, Improve Your Self-Confidence and Communication Skills to Establish New Relationships.

Blake Sullivan

Table of Contents

INTRODUCTION

Effective communication has become critical for success in both personal and professional contexts in today's fast-paced and linked world. Whether you're networking at a business conference, striking up a conversation with a new acquaintance, or simply trying to connect with someone on a deeper level, the ability to talk to anybody with ease and confidence can open up countless opportunities and enrich your life in meaningful ways.

But for many people, starting a conversation with a stranger can be intimidating or overwhelming. They may struggle with shyness, social anxiety, or a lack of confidence in their own communication skills, leading to missed opportunities and a sense of isolation. This book is for you if you could use a little help when communicating with others. In *How to Talk to Anybody with Confidence,* we'll explore the art of effective communication and provide practical strategies and tools for building your confidence, overcoming your fears, and connecting with anyone, anywhere. Drawing on the latest research in psychology, neuroscience, and interpersonal communication, this book will help you:

- Develop the mindset of a confident communicator

- Start conversations with ease and grace

- Connect with others on a deeper level

- Build rapport and trust quickly

- Overcome social anxiety and shyness

- Navigate difficult conversations with ease

- And much more!

Whether you're looking to advance your career, expand your social circle, or simply become a more confident and engaging communicator, How to Talk to Anybody is the ultimate guide to mastering the art of conversation and unlocking your full potential. So if you're ready to take your communication skills to the next level, prepare to immerse yourself in the pages that follow and, in the words of Sir Winston Churchill, *"Courage is what it takes to stand up and speak; courage is also what it takes to sit down and listen."*

Have a good read,

Blake Sullivan

Chapter 1: Social Issues

We all long for meaningful connections with others, yet sometimes our efforts to relate can be met with roadblocks and setbacks. Whether it's a struggle to make friends, conflicts with loved ones, or feeling like we don't fit in, problems relating can be a source of deep pain and frustration. If you face challenges in your relationships, know you're not alone. Many people struggle with problems relating at various points in their lives, and it's okay to feel overwhelmed or uncertain about navigating these difficulties.

In this chapter, we'll explore some common challenges people face when relating and offer insight and strategies for overcoming them. We'll discuss social anxiety, trust issues, communication problems, and more topics and provide practical tips for building more satisfying and fulfilling relationships. While problems in relating can be tough to face, they also offer growth and learning opportunities. By confronting these challenges head-on, we can gain a deeper understanding of ourselves and others and develop the skills and resilience we need to build stronger, more meaningful connections. Let's find out together what the most common social problems are; only by giving them a definition will we be able to gain awareness to solve them.

Social Anxiety

Sufferers of this disorder deeply fear social situations, particularly when these involve potential judgment. The individual's fear is of acting or showing signs of anxiety in a humiliating or embarrassing way. And thus to blush, sweat, tremble, stumble in speech, show oneself awkward, weak, and incapable.

Underlying social phobia is the disproportionate concern that one's internal anxious experience may be noticed and judged, causing embarrassment. The public manifestation of one's anxiety takes the form of the individual's inability to align with social demands. This results in shame. Each feared situation causes unmanageable anxiety, endured with great effort and discomfort, or avoided altogether. Inevitable experiences, even if the person realizes the disproportionality of their fears.

So does being easily embarrassed in public situations mean suffering from Social Anxiety? Absolutely not. When we have to expose ourselves to a public situation or the judgment of others, many people experience feeling a little more awkward or inadequate. These are frequent and normal emotional manifestations that may reflect personal temperaments or reactions to specific conditions. As always, underlying the definition of the disorder, the intensity factor is very important. The symptoms of Social Anxiety are such that they significantly impair the individual's social or work life.

What contexts trigger Social Anxiety Disorder?

The contexts that trigger Social Anxiety Disorder can be either performance or interaction. Both are conditions of exposure to social justice. It may be critical for the person to speak in front of an audience but also to use public transportation, to write or sign a document under the gaze of others, to go to a party or movie theater, or simply, to wait in line for one's turn to do something. When the fears include most social interactions, we speak of Generalized Social Phobia.

Causes & Diagnosis of Social Anxiety

It is not always easy to determine the specific incidence of Social Anxiety Disorder. It, in fact, often occurs in conjunction with other disorders and is rarely diagnosed alone. It is often mistakenly superimposed on interpersonal patterns of shyness and avoidance.

Social Anxiety Disorder, as well as other phobic-based anxiety disorders, appears to be due to several factors, both genetic predisposition and environmental what this means.

Where a predisposition is present, some specific life experiences (usually experienced during childhood) may contribute to triggering Social Anxiety Disorder. These negative activating experiences often concern the judgment of others, experienced critically and destructively.

Depression

Depression represents one of the pathologies in the landscape of psychiatric diseases, which tends to have numerous "shades," levels of severity, and symptoms. Because of this, therapeutic and psychopharmacological protocols change from person to person, and treatment and improvements are subjective and manifest themselves with different timing from patient to patient.

One aspect often present and falls within the framework of "Depression" is social isolation. The depressed patient typically presents with a symptom set characterized by depressed mood, feelings of sadness, low drive and energy, loss of pleasure in what used to interest him/her, and poor participation with loved ones.

Already this first symptomatological picture can set the stage for a progressive reduction of interest in social life to set in; the anergic, sad, numb patient will tend to close in on himself and not seek out affection; often, these patients spend much of their day "in bed," I am often told: *"...not to feel the weight of my thoughts... "or "...I can't even get out of bed... I don't feel like doing anything anymore; nothing makes sense..."*

Another aspect that leads to social withdrawal is the condition of illness that often leads the patient to *"not require the presence of other people"* or *"...I stay alone... I am afraid that others will see me like this..."*

Still another aspect related to social isolation is the alteration of the affective sphere, which often no longer turns out to be adherent to reality. Very often, the patient does not feel understood by the family members or thinks that he is bothering the family members, or in the most severe cases, there is a kind of " affectivity" towards the loved ones, that is, an inability to feel those feelings of depression were present and alive. This sphere of social withdrawal should not be underestimated because when it goes to establish itself, it is synonymous with an already complicated depressive picture, which must absolutely be taken into consideration and subjected to the appropriate treatment; this is because the picture can go on to complicate further or then lay the groundwork for a possible chronicization of the disease.

Past Traumas

Traumatic events are those that jeopardize a person's physical or mental well-being. Some individuals who have encountered terrible events develop post-traumatic stress disorder (PTSD). The physiological response to stimuli, panic attacks, chronic anxiety, feelings of anger or numbness, or a lack of confidence are only a few of the trauma-related symptoms experienced by many more people.

In addition to direct experiences of trauma like rape, childhood abuse, or military combat, people can develop trauma-like reactions and susceptibility to emotional activation and reactivity from an accumulation of negative life events, chronic unresolved stress (such as prolonged unemployment), previous abusive relationships, or growing up in a dysfunctional family.

Trauma therapists commonly refer to these experiences as "small T traumas" instead of "big T traumas," which relate to events that seriously threaten one's life. Both can devastate relationships if left untreated by therapy or self-help. Below are five ways in which trauma can negatively affect relationships:

Fight, flight, or freeze

Your brain can enter a "fight, flight, or freeze" state if you haven't dealt with traumatic experiences or severe, ongoing, chronic stressors, which hijack basic networks involved in survival and threat response.

The amygdala is responsible for generating the "fight," "flight," or "freeze" response in response to a perceived threat to one's social relationships, and if you had to use one of these responses as a child to survive (such as running away from a borderline parent or fighting a drunk, angry parent so he wouldn't hurt a younger sibling), your brain would give preference to that response type from now on. It can lead to the following behaviors that are detrimental to relationships:

- **Fighting.** Abusive behavior includes hitting or yelling at the other person, blaming them for everything wrong in your life, treating them with disdain, being overly bossy, and refusing to let things go.

- **Flighting.** Trying to get away from a close person or a difficult situation, acting impulsively out of fear, or trying to avoid dealing with a problem by running away.

- **Freezing.** Having a lack of control over one's life, feeling helpless, or withdrawing emotionally from one's loved ones.

Vergence-based responses

Toxic guilt can develop in response to prolonged social rejection or trauma. It's well-known that shame can wreck relationships (unless you have actually done something terrible). When humiliated, you may want to withdraw from society or take your frustration out on those you hold responsible. You feel like you need to keep vital secrets from your partner. You can build a "wall" around yourself and hide your weaknesses by attacking others or overcompensating for your own shortcomings.

If you're feeling guilty, it's hard to take in criticism, no matter how well-meaning the critic may be. You'll likely take a defensive stance because you don't want your flaws highlighted. When people feel ashamed, they prefer to give up on their relationships rather than fight for them.

To cope with your guilt, you may turn to unhealthy, compulsive behaviors. You may tend to compulsive behavior, such as excessive drinking or drug use, gaming, shopping, sexual activity, or work.

Being Triggered in States of Trauma

Situations that trigger memories of the initial trauma, the ongoing stressor, or situations that your brain determines are crucial for your physical or emotional survival can trigger "fight, flight, or freeze" reactions in people with unresolved trauma or PTSD (Post Traumatic Stress Disorder) symptoms who regularly face stressful situations.

Because our forebears lived in tribes and relied on them for protection, sustenance, and protection, we are hardwired to treat rejection and desertion in romantic relationships as if they were actual risks to our physical well-being. You are more likely to react to marital conflict or rejection by activating the brain's initial survival processes if you have a history of trauma or are currently in a particularly unsafe situation (due to debt, unemployment, or significant disease, for example).

The amygdala takes over and triggers fight, flight or freeze responses when the brain classifies a problem in a relationship as a threat to survival. Because of this, you may start shouting, losing your temper, or closing down emotionally. Your partner's network of emergency responses may be activated, and the cycle will continue if you respond in any of these ways.

Rigid and unfavorable relationship beliefs

Relationship trauma or dysfunctional family history that hasn't been addressed can have a lasting negative impact on your perspective of relationships. Then, because of your beliefs, you can interpret the behavior of people around you in the most negative way. If you're constantly checking in on your friends or trying to exert too much authority over them, it could be because you lack trust in them.

As a result of an irrational fear of rejection or abandonment, you may avoid putting yourself out there to meet new people and broaden your circle of friends and loved ones. You may be under the impression that your significant other will never be able to meet your expectations or feel motivated to do so. Since your friends may not appreciate your efforts to explain your feelings and needs, you may develop resentment.

Those with unresolved trauma are likelier to pick and stick with toxic partners. Family trauma, whether severe (the "big T") or mild (the "small T"), can leave you feeling insecure and unworthy of affection. If you put up with disrespect from your partner, you may be less likely to draw boundaries or end the relationship.

People often stay in toxic relationships because they're afraid to be alone more than they are of their abuser. It is possible to be overly self-conscious, self-critical, and vulnerable to outside influences (as you were by your dysfunctional parent). Addiction to emotional intensity brought on by trauma bonding can cause you to favor unreliable people, rejecting, demeaning, or manipulative over those who are nice, honest, and respectful. Because of this, you might be more likely to choose partners who are abusive or uncaring.

Low Self-Esteem

To know yourself, to love yourself, and to have self-esteem, is the basis of relationships. Self-awareness is the basis of self-esteem. Self-esteem is not a generic "I am worth," as some product advertisements would have us believe. To achieve self-esteem, we must first know ourselves thoroughly: be able to describe ourselves precisely in all areas that affect us, starting with our physical appearance, cognitive abilities, ways of relating and communicating, managing and expressing emotions, and ending with our bodily experience and sexuality. We cannot estimate something that we cannot even see for what it is. It is the first brick of self-esteem.

The second brick is to estimate the importance of the characteristics we find in ourselves. For example, if I do not have a French nose, but I value having it important, this will affect my self-esteem. That is, self-esteem should build primarily on our strengths and values/interests. As for the weaknesses-points, it is certainly important to improve them if they are valuable to us, but not if they are valuable to others Self-esteem, therefore, is formed as a result of knowing and accurately assessing one's abilities and limitations and accepting both.

Yet this process of knowledge, evaluation, to acceptance of self is by no means taken for granted. Why?

Because often, while growing up, this delicate process is disturbed by external expectations and criticism that push the child to conform to the wishes of others and not to be as they really are becoming. So our self-assessment barometer goes haywire, and instead of listening to what our own experience tells us to build our own idea of ourselves, others, and the world, we give credence to the judgments of others. Why is it difficult to have satisfying relationships without good self-esteem?

- Because without self-esteem, we tend to look to others for the basis of our acceptance

- Because if we do not know our needs, we cannot know who will be compatible with their fulfillment

- Because if we do not treat ourselves with love, we will find people who will do the same for us

- Because only if we know ourselves are we able to make clear demands of each other

Those with low self-esteem have negative expectations of their lives: they get anxious, limit their experiences and make little effort (thinking thereby to mitigate the effects of failures); but in doing so, they do not get what they want (they increase failures) and thus do not nurture self-esteem.

On the other hand, those with good self-esteem have positive expectations of their lives, so they work as hard as they need to and experience anxiety appropriate to the situation. By doing so, people get what they want more easily; even if they do not always get what they want, they know how to learn from mistakes and objectively evaluate what happened. In short, they know how to see what is useful to them and overlook what is only harmful. *How to develop or improve self-esteem?* It is necessary to:

- Having a precise and detailed knowledge of oneself

- Committing to what really interests us (if I aspire to something that does not match my values or is beyond my abilities/possibilities, I will likely have self-esteem problems)

- Knowing how to attribute the results of our successes to ourselves

- Knowing that striving for perfection will most likely lead to never being satisfied with ourselves

It is necessary to move from confused dissatisfaction to precise awareness by asking oneself:

- In what areas am I satisfied, and in what areas am I dissatisfied with myself?

- What are the causes of these dissatisfactions?

- What can I do to change this situation of dissatisfaction? Do I need someone's help?

You may have problems with self-esteem if:

- You focus much more on your mistakes and failures and much less on your abilities and successes.

- If you tend to live with your attention focused excessively on the past or the future instead of working to improve your present

- If you feel inadequate, you think you do not deserve happiness.

In this chapter, we have explored several common problems that can lead to poor social skills, including social anxiety, depression, past traumas, and low self-esteem. These challenges can be deeply impactful, making it difficult to connect with others, form meaningful relationships, and feel comfortable in social situations. It's important to remember that change takes time and effort and that setbacks and obstacles are a normal part of the process. But by staying committed to our goals, seeking help when needed, and practicing self-compassion and self-care, we can develop the skills and resilience we need to thrive in our social lives.

So if you're struggling with social anxiety, depression, past traumas, or low self-esteem, know there is hope for a brighter future. With determination, patience, and a willingness to learn and grow, you can overcome these challenges and build relationships that bring joy, connection, and fulfillment into your life.

Chapter 2: How to 10x Your Social Skills

Social skills are an essential part of our daily lives. Our ability to connect and interact with others is critical in our personal and professional relationships. However, social situations can be anxiety-inducing and uncomfortable for many people, leading to isolation and loneliness. This chapter will explore some effective techniques for developing and enhancing your social skills. We understand that working on this can be a sensitive and personal topic, and we want you to know that we approach this subject with empathy and understanding. Our goal is to help you develop the tools and strategies you need to build meaningful relationships that bring joy and fulfillment to your life.

So if you're ready to take the next step in your journey toward improved social skills, let's get started. Together, we'll explore practical techniques and strategies that you can use to develop the skills and confidence you need to thrive in social situations and create strong and meaningful relationships.

The Importance of Self-Confidence in Social Environments

Self-confidence is the knowledge that we can rely on ourselves first and foremost as people worthy of worth. Esteeming ourselves means not questioning our importance and, as a result, being able to take responsibility for others. A healthy relationship begins with treating each other with the respect they deserve. Most people don't give much thought to the consequences of their actions, but when respect is lacking, it significantly impacts all of one's relationships.

In fact, the belief that we are worthy of esteem imprints our entire relationship with the environment and influences its interpretation and perception. Strong self-esteem allows one to deal with problematic situations assertively, avoiding interpreting them as crippling, with no way out, or as intolerable provocations.

Coming out of the confines of the usual definitions, what does self-esteem really mean? Where does it come from? Does a person possess good self-esteem because it is an inherent character characteristic, or do his genes determine it? If I have low self-esteem, am I destined to live with this perception for the rest of my life, or can I do something to change it? Here are some very common and important questions.

Every action (or failed action) is subject to subjective evaluation. One's evaluation happens almost automatically; hardly a person is really aware of it or pauses to reflect on it unless one is prompted to do so or stimulated to reframe the initial judgment. And it is precisely the immediacy with which we often judge ourselves, our relationships, and others that leads one to think that this way of thinking is consistent with one's own person, emotions, and aspirations and consequently does not need any critical revision.

However, one's own value system, what everyone believes and feels to be authentic, important, and true, is often nothing more than a cage that one's history of experiences has led one to build around. It is not easy to be aware of how much this cage a person lives with for years can limit one's social development and relationships. It is painful to see how people capable of worth limit themselves in every aspiration and self-expression, locked in a prison of severity and self-punishment justified by the belief that the outside world would never accept them as they really are. But convinced by whom and by what?

In the imagination of many, everyone is worthy of esteeming themselves the closer they come, as a way of life and thinking, to a winning protagonist of the real or fantasy life of the soap opera of the moment or the news report of some television star. After years of exposure to the false world of the media, the confusion between external and superficial factors and more fundamental aspects makes it difficult to understand who one really is and what good and true characteristics to base one's self-esteem on. In attempting to achieve imposed standards and make oneself another person, the belief that the person one is is unacceptable is increasingly reinforced. Self-esteem is linked to recognizing oneself as one is and not as one learns to pretend to be. Low confidence produces:

- Low confidence in oneself and the world;

- The difficulty of listening to oneself and identifying realistic goals consistent with one's aspirations;

- The lack of a personal life project;

- The tendency to react impulsively instead of thinking about what you want and what you are;

- The inability to take full responsibility for one's life;

- The failure to recognize one's right to freely and fully manifest oneself;

- The tendency to depend on others to define one's worth as a person and one's abilities;

- The pursuit of others' consent, poor initiative, and unwillingness to take risks;

- Fear of taking responsibility for one's own behavior constructively and positively.

Self-esteem affects the very personal conception of success. Success is no longer understood as a positive outcome for one's own goal and one's own system of resources and constraints, but rather as falling within norms of behavior and values typical of the social network to which one belongs (i.e., becoming "the way you want me"). The judgment of others becomes a source of anxiety, especially when associated with the fear of losing social esteem and approval, making it crucial to comply with the more or less explicit norms of the group to which one belongs. Such an attitude undermines the person's self-image and is dysfunctional for personal development itself because it does not allow one to learn to give importance to what may be appropriate for each person and to choose thoughts and behaviors consistent with one's own characteristics and potential. Feeling the pleasure of being oneself and succeeding in asserting oneself as one means not posing towards one's reality passively and not investing time and resources to please people in one's relational environment. It means being assertive, that is, creating communications and relationships that are respectful of one's own emotions and needs while respecting the needs and rights of others. Learning to handle contact with people assertively means dealing with others in a balanced way and feeling less conditioned by the fear of not being liked or of being dispossessed of rights and spaces that instead belong to us. The path to assertiveness starts with developing the ability to interpret situations as they arise, having as a reference your rights and those of your interlocutor. And it is important to train our ability to defend and support them even when the temptation to let go is very strong.

Practical Strategies to Improve Self-Confidence

It is an ingredient that should not be missing to succeed in life and achieve one's goals. Of course, I'm talking about self-confidence. You must have failed at one time or another. Maybe in your job, maybe in some university exam, or maybe the person you loved let you down deeply. How did you react?

This question represents a real test of how much confidence you have in yourself. If you stop and think about it, in fact, some people react to failures by getting back up and also looking at positive aspects and people who shut down and get depressed. On what does this depend? On the confidence we have in ourselves.

The modern world allows few people to have strong self-confidence. Many people ask for more and more self-confidence without ever looking for a limit. But is this always the case? Why do some people always seem to have self-confidence?

Let us try to break a spear towards those who have little confidence and try to create and build it daily, admiring those who, on the other hand, always seem to have confidence. Let us assume that in new situations, any person has to deal with a physiological reaction with increased adrenaline and an attack-escape reaction. This attack-escape reaction makes anyone who is affected by it anxious. It means that such a spontaneous physiological reaction in our body puts anyone in crisis when faced with a new situation.

What some people have over others is the ability to handle highly tense situations, such as a change in one's life, without shaking one's self-esteem and self-confidence, making oneself strong in the eyes of others. Here is a list of 5 tools for improving self-confidence:

1) Regain the peace of mind you deserve

After going through a bad period, it is normal to feel moral down or not have the usual peace of mind in facing everyday life, but sooner or later, you have to find the courage to pick yourself up and start again. Some responsive people roll up their sleeves to forget difficult times, making resilience a valuable ally. Not familiar with this term?

Resilience, in psychology, means the ability to cope positively with traumatic events, showing enthusiasm toward the opportunities that life holds for us. Being peaceful means feeling fulfilled and satisfied while knowing that life is not always rosy.

Try to file away negative experiences, relax as soon as possible by doing some sports, appreciate your peculiarities, hang out with people who make you feel good, and focus on the things you enjoy.

2) Live new experiences

According to recent research conducted in the United States, what kills self-confidence is a habit. A life, to be truly fulfilling and satisfying, should not be based on the possession of material goods but instead on experiences. Traveling, studying, and learning about new realities are essential to increase one's cultural background and gain more self-confidence.

The real killer of happiness and self-actualization seems almost paradoxically to be money. Imagine a typical situation: the desire to buy something expensive, such as a pair of designer shoes, the latest smartphone model, or a luxurious car.

Once you make the purchase, you feel happy and fulfilled, but later on, the habit will take over, and possess that good will make you lose even the sense of happiness attached to it. Identify your passions and always seek new stimuli; you may discover really curious aspects of yourself!

3) Manage negative emotions

The first step in defeating negative emotions is to identify them exactly. When you experience a strange feeling, you need to stop for a moment and reflect and figure out what is wrong. Have you experienced anger or displeasure? Did you get nervous or feel a state of anxiety?

After this preliminary stage, you will have to identify the trigger, the spring that caused that behavior in you: who did what to you, where and when it happened.

The second stage requires introspective work on analyzing your own thoughts. Why did you feel that way at that time? What created suffering or discomfort for you? Finally, you will have to try your best to change the negative thoughts, accepting and metabolizing them. To help you on this complex path of personal growth, you might write everything down in a journal.

4) Take a positive attitude

Positive thinking is a mental attitude that sees favorable outcomes in every circumstance, a process that can transform positive energy into reality. A person who relates enthusiastically to life will have more self-confidence, whether in the professional or private sphere, than someone who sees everything in a traumatic way.

To truly feel good and cope with life's difficulties every day, it is necessary to have a positive mental attitude. This alternative spirit will help us face new challenges and achieve new goals with serenity and confidence, thus with a greater chance of success. How to maintain a positive attitude even on a "black" day?

It's all a matter of practice: "positive thinking" is not always the solution to problems, but certainly a very useful mental approach. Below you will find a few small tricks:

- Always start the day thinking about the positive aspects of your work;

- Think about the people who love you, always ready to offer you their support;

- Focus on what you could learn from even the most disastrous experiences;

- Avoid quarrelsome people or confrontational situations;

- Convey your positive emotions: such an attitude will propagate and be absorbed by others, which will be well-disposed toward you.

5) Take care of yourself

How many times have you heard this beautiful phrase repeated? Taking care of yourself sounds so easy in words, a concept almost taken for granted nowadays. Yet, if we stop and think carefully about what has just been said, we might observe that it is not straightforward to put yourself first, pamper yourself and carve out the right spaces for yourself every day. Taking care of oneself means really listening to the needs of one's body and indulging them so that the right level of physical well-being is guaranteed.

The same goes for our soul: it is constantly speaking to us, guiding us to do what is best for us and others; it knows when it is time to give and when it is time to receive when it is time to be in a company or solitude. The real problem is to begin to listen to its voice and give it the importance it deserves. Here are some helpful tips:

- Carve out the time you need to rest;

- Practice the sport you enjoy most;

- Reserve a special gift from time to time;

- Ask yourself if what you are doing reflects your needs truly.

6) Don't compare yourself to others

If you want to gain more self-confidence, you must stop seeking constant comparison with others. Unfortunately, the perfectionism that modern society pushes us toward is not positive for one's self-esteem. On a psychological level, healthy comparison can act as a stimulus, but when it exceeds the limit of normality, it induces people to demand more and more of themselves, with a stress load that is very difficult to bear.

This behavior could prove debilitating and prevent you from living with serenity and balance. Learn to resist the need to compare yourself to others by becoming aware of your great gifts. Appreciate yourself for who you really are, as a unique and special being. Leave more room for collaboration and less for competition; I am sure you will reap many benefits in your private and work spheres. Instead of envying others, commit to increasing your knowledge and skills.

How to Talk Confidently

Speaking with confidence will lead others to have more confidence in us and to think of us as intelligent people, especially when it comes to public speaking. Knowing how to speak with confidence, therefore, could enable us to achieve success, especially professionally. What should be done, however, to make this confidence our own? What can we do to win the confidence of others? Below we share some key aspects that will help you speak confidently. One thing is certain; you need a lot of practice.

1. State your opinions with a belief

Before we speak, we must believe in what we say. It is the only way we will convey our conviction and will for others to participate in our ideas. It is paramount, however, not to be arrogant when we do so. We must not display an attitude that reveals a need for approval or validation but rather show conviction.

2. The importance of eye contact

Eye contact is, first of all, a sign of good manners toward others. On the other hand, it will cause the audience to listen more attentively to what we are saying and immerse themselves in our speech.

We will also be able to express our message more clearly and increase our self-confidence. Looking to the floor, to the ceiling, or no one, in particular will make us feel more insecure, and our listeners will understand that.

It, however, does not mean that we should only focus on one person since, in addition to making them uncomfortable, we will be distracted. A good method can be to turn our gaze to a different person every three seconds, looking into their eyes.

We should not worry if we notice that someone in our audience is confused or worried. It may weaken our self-confidence. Finally, if we are speaking to a large audience, it is ideal to direct our gaze to only one group of people.

3. Recognizing your own worth

In addition to showing others that we have confidence in ourselves, speaking with confidence originates from a deep love for ourselves. For this, it will be essential to know our virtues. However, we must be careful. Vanity and arrogance will reign against us.

One way to increase self-confidence can be to praise ourselves daily. In this way, self-confidence can be conveyed in our speeches and will be easily perceived by others. Focus on what you are good at or the aspects you value most about yourself. Praise yourself without thinking about your shortcomings.

4. Expand your vocabulary

Read as much as you can, from online magazines to serious literature. In addition to expanding your vocabulary, expanding your knowledge base is a direct result of reading widely. In no time, you'll be using the new vocabulary and idioms you've picked up in your everyday speech. You cannot have a restricted vocabulary if you are really intent on speaking well. It does not mean you must spend a fortune on books for your speeches or daily conversations. Already a few more "researched" words may make you sound smarter to your interlocutor's ears, but they will not give the impression that you are trying hard.

Write the words down in a notebook. Jot down any new words you encounter as you read and write down their definition.

5. Don't be afraid of pauses

Some people see pauses as a sign of weakness, but this is untrue. It is okay to pause to gather your thoughts and mentally formulate the sentence to be spoken next. It is much worse to speak too fast and give the impression of rushing, being flustered, or even saying something you may regret later. In your speech, you should not speak fast but reflectively: only then will the pauses be natural.

Don't stress too much if you use pauses (such as "um," or "uhm") in your speech. It's just a way of "shifting into mental gear," Even leading politicians and diplomats use them frequently. If you feel you use them too often, you can try to make an effort to decrease them, but there is no need to avoid them altogether.

How to Build Emotional Resilience

Every day brings new, challenging obstacles, but how we deal with them matters most. The ability to avoid them has the potential to alter one's existence completely. Remember those days when you dread going to work because of the mounting pressure you'll feel when you open your eyes? The kids can't find their backpacks, the trains are running late, and to cap it all off, your boss sends you an email demanding a report by 9:30 a.m.

All of us can relate to that feeling. While some people can avoid the blows and keep cool, others instantly feel stressed and remain so for the rest of the day. Our stress tolerance varies according to the difficulties we encounter at home and in the workplace. Our mutual reaction helps us stay at peace with one another. Bouncing back quickly from emotional setbacks is crucial in a world where stress can be triggered by anything. Having excellent self-management skills is essential to emotional resilience. It's about making decisions that help you persevere when things get tough. Many people have told me, "I am just not resilient." The good news is that resilience can be trained like any other muscle. The more you use your brain, the stronger it will become. Here is a guide to building emotional resilience:

1. Accept yourself

One of the most crucial elements of resilience is developing an unconditional sense of self-acceptance or simply becoming at ease in one's own skin. Living in a social media bubble and having unreal expectations in today's "likes and clicks" society is easy.

Put an end to constant self-evaluation concerning others and shift your attention from flaws to strengths. Consistently focusing on your positive qualities in written affirmations. Put together a daily log of three things and post it where you can see it daily. Bring about more of the good and fewer of the bad.

2. Direct your Energy to attention

Our minds are predisposed to see the worst in situations, so it's important to train ourselves to look on the bright side. The secret to maintaining a positive outlook is to "make noise" about your achievements rather than ruminating on your setbacks. When I make a mistake, instead of beating myself up about it, I try to see it as a chance to grow as a person.

3. Learn to let go

Emotionally resilient people understand that being right all the time isn't a prerequisite for happiness. It's nice to win an argument, but winning the war for happiness is much more important. By abandoning the belief that others owe you their undying adoration, gratitude, and admiration, you'll find that your rigid outlook on life begins to loosen up considerably. Consider how modifying your reactions could lead to personal development.

To develop emotional distance, practices like mindfulness and meditation are invaluable. If you're looking for a way to practice mindfulness, try doing something you enjoy that also helps you unwind and stop overthinking: cooking, walking, gardening, etc.

4. Put yourself on your to-do list

A commitment to self-care is essential if you want to build up your emotional resilience and make it a permanent part of your life. Making a vow to better yourself emotionally is a powerful practice. Self-care is paramount, so prioritize it.

5. Gratitude is the attitude

Gratitude helps set the tone for my day, so I try to practice it every morning. Every morning before I have my first cup of coffee, I take a moment to reflect on the three things for which I am most thankful. Feeling grateful helps one see things more clearly. It's much more challenging to complain and be pessimistic when we can acknowledge the positives and the negatives. The mind is reprogrammed to be more optimistic and grateful for what it has. Keeping a gratitude journal is a wonderful way to keep track of the people and experiences for which you are grateful.

6. It's good to be kind

My dad always told me that kindness is a virtue, and he was right; it does one's spirit some good. Those feel-good endorphins are released when we help others, so it's no surprise that this makes us happy. Volunteers experience greater happiness, according to research conducted at the London School of Economics. Nonetheless, small acts of kindness can go a long way; just give a stranger a friendly smile or a sincere compliment.

Finding what works for you and making that part of your daily routine is crucial for building emotional resilience.

Build Meaningful Relationships

In the most difficult times, relationships can help us. People with a good network of interpersonal relationships derive more satisfaction, enjoy better health, and experience greater well-being.

Autonomy, a sense of independence, and being on one's own are often extolled as crucial factors for healthy development and as the final landing point for maturity. Being autonomous and able to direct one's life and choices is necessary, but aspiring to complete autonomy from the world of relationships in the hope that it will be the key to one's fulfillment can lead to misunderstandings.

We are social beings; we need to live within a system of relationships where exchanges and sharing make experiences more meaningful and profound.

Positive relationships are one of the most relevant protective factors for our mental health and psychic balance; they satisfy us when there is mutual interest and care, respect, and consideration. In them, we trust, energize and enable us to live in synergy with others, giving them the energy we receive, satisfying our desire to help and support each other, to see and be seen with loving, compassionate, and kind eyes.

Maintaining connections with others is vital for every human being, but not all relationships provide the same protection and tutelage. Some can be disturbing and destructive: these are the toxic relationships that can harm, create upset, cross boundaries, and lead to antagonism.

Fostering and cultivating positive relationships requires commitment and flexibility. Whether it is a time of loneliness, reconstruction, or transition, we can find ourselves experiencing moments of loneliness and isolation. In these hard times, we need to be creative and strategic in identifying people to be with, and this search requires attention, commitment, and effort. Finding people with whom we can establish bonds of authentic attunement can also mean doing some pruning, letting go of old patterns of behavior that belong to the past, and stopping hanging out with people who, instead of moving us forward, mortify us. We must open ourselves to possibilities about what we want our relationships to represent.

During this stage, fear can make room within us when we put ourselves out there searching for new interpersonal relationships. We may hesitate to describe our internal state of loneliness and worry, wondering if it is safe to open up if we are the only ones experiencing that problem. Will the other person be able to listen to me? Will they consider me a stupid person once I confide? Will people think I am strange?

It is important to have a group of people to refer to who can instill confidence, energy, and support, which are essential for our mental well-being. Here are three words that identify some of the characteristics that people who stand by us should have:

- **Trust:** people who listen without judgment, see you as you are, and want the best for you. Empathetic people who give you constructive, caring feedback. People you can be yourself with and rely on.

- **Energy**: people who motivate and inspire you, who think creatively and innovatively. Who give you new and useful points of view and observation to navigate complexity. Who is fun, and with whom do you have fun? Most of all, they make you grow and value you.

- **Mentors:** people who encourage you to believe in your abilities and use them to the best of your ability, willing to share their points of view as you grow. Who helps you recognize your capacities for growth, development adaptation, and resilience.

Some suggestions for building a network of relationships that will help you grow and improve your well-being:

- Think about your target group. What are the people there within your family? Who do you refer to in times of difficulty? To your group of friends or work or other groups?

- When you find yourself in a new circumstance, try to identify people who can become meaningful reference points. You must try to take the risk of stepping up and coming out of the closet a bit to start building relationships and trust. Chances are this will happen: peer support is a protective factor for mental health.

- Set boundaries. If someone has an attitude or behaviors that are not beneficial or not helping you feel good, be clear and try to communicate how you feel and renegotiate and change certain dynamics if possible. Remove yourself from that situation if you don't feel it is worth it. Perhaps clear boundaries need to be established for unhealthy relationships.

- Tune into the frequencies of trust. Are your boundaries too thick, or are they too labile? Are you dealing with past disappointments? Does social anxiety or insecurity make it difficult for you to open up and build mutual trust? Do you tend to trust too easily?

- Use the resources you can access: if you feel it would help at a time of transition, you can seek the support or advocacy of a psychologist.

- Be patient and diligent. Even if things don't go well right away, be patient. You can't fit in with just anyone. Finding the right fit in relationships takes time. Stay resilient and make sure that past negative experiences don't affect you and cause you to think that no one can be worthy of your trust: doing so would actually risk never finding the emotional connection you are looking for. It takes time.

In times of change and challenge, we need each other; having a reference group that represents interchange can help you build lasting, protective relationships and help you improve your well-being. While building meaningful relationships may not always be easy, the benefits that come with it are invaluable. An individual's sense of community, safety, and contentment can all increase due to having strong bonds with other people. They can also help us learn and grow as individuals and open up new opportunities in our personal and professional lives. Ultimately, prioritizing and investing in building meaningful relationships can create a richer, more fulfilling life for ourselves and those around us.

How to Develop a Positive Mindset

Let's face it: positive thinking, so much in the 1990s, has lost credibility over time and has become synonymous with dull, unmotivated optimism. As if positive thinkers are people who do not see problems or pretend that everything is fine while the world around them falls apart.

In reality, positive thinking began as a productive approach to difficulties and unpleasant situations. If we are worried about a problem, our worries will limit our actions and possible solutions. It happens because we are not good at handling the emotions generated by stressful situations. Conversely, on the other hand, if we maintain a positive attitude toward the problem in front of us, the range of possible solutions expands because we can see the bigger picture and project ourselves into a scenario where we have already overcome the obstacle.

But is it really possible to control thoughts and prevent negative ones from conditioning our reality? Of course not, and this is one of the reasons why positive thinking theories have been much criticized. In addition, there is another element to consider: negative thoughts are not as harmful as people think. Let's start with an assumption: thoughts are products of our mind and have a neutral value. They represent how our rationality reacts to certain circumstances and processes our emotions. There is a gulf between thinking and doing, and often thoughts, even the darkest ones, vanish without doing any damage. One fact that remains to condition our thoughts is our mindset, forma mentis. If you have a personal narrative that you are an unlucky person to whom everything goes wrong, you will read every event from this perspective. That is why today, alongside positive thinking, we combine building a positive mindset with a winning combination.

Having a positive mindset enhances positive thinking

How is positive thinking enhanced by having a positive mindset? Simplifying a lot, we could say that positive thinking is about generating optimistic and confident thoughts regardless of objective reality. If you are faced with a problem, you will cultivate the thought that everything will surely be all right, one way or another. The positive mindset is primarily focused on action. If you are faced with that same problem, you analyze the situation and focus on what you can do to overcome the difficulties. The sine qua non for cultivating a positive mindset is having a good regard for your worth. If you trust your abilities, you will also trust the effectiveness of your actions.

How can you cultivate a positive mindset?

- **Train your motivation with music.** Music accompanies us through our days by acting as an echo or background to our moods. But we can also use it to charge us positively. Make a playlist of all the songs that make you feel active and invigorated, predispose you to action, and channel your energy constructively. Listen to your playlist right in the morning or when you feel sluggish. Your day will have a different spirit.
- **Train your motivation with journaling.** Try the Five Minute Journal. It is a journal that takes you 5 minutes a day and sets you up as early as the morning to decide the direction of your day. If you are consistent, at some point, you will feel that you have the reins of your life in your hands and decide where to direct it. In addition, focusing on the little good things to remember about the day is an exercise in positivity.
- **Spend time on your passions.** People who can value their passions are more confident in their worth. In addition, shifting our focus from a potentially problematic activity to a fun one helps us

return to our routine, recharged, and with fresh ideas. And what better way to cultivate a positive mindset than to look at the problem with fresh eyes?

- **Turn your inner dialogue into a positive one.** Being critical of yourself does not help the mindset and tends to be a self-sabotaging mechanism. How do you talk to yourself differently? By avoiding quick judgments and keeping yourself open to broader possibilities. If you didn't get that job, telling yourself you are incompetent does little good. Instead, suggesting to yourself that you could deepen skills on which you feel weak has much more constructive value. Instead of telling yourself phrases like "I'll never make it," try turning them into positives: "I'll work hard to make it." It is not about self-conviction but a change of perspective.

- **Surround yourself with positive people.** Since no man is an island, the people we associate with greatly impact our well-being and condition our mindset. If surrounded by friends and acquaintances with a proactive attitude, we will naturally be inclined to formulate our thoughts positively. Therefore, it would be best to limit hanging out with people who drain our energy with complaints and an ever-pessimistic outlook.

Chapter 3: Communication 101

Possessing good communication skills is crucial to making oneself understood by others and establishing good interpersonal relationships. It also affects our self-esteem and deploys well for those who exercise leadership within the social group to which they belong.

It may seem like a simple phenomenon, but it actually consists of many elements and requires specific skills to be truly effective. It is possible, in fact, to be misunderstood or not understand what is being said to us. Communication, moreover, is a tool that must be used judiciously, taking care not to convey messages of a sexist, homophobic nature or that can harm the other person.

This chapter will explore the various forms of communication and their definitions. By understanding these, we can gain a deeper appreciation for the importance of effective communication in our daily lives. This knowledge can also help us to improve our communication skills, allowing us to better connect with others and achieve our personal and professional goals.

Definition

Communication is an *"interactive exchange between at least two participants, who mutually have communicative intention and awareness, and who share a given meaning based on conventional symbolic and signaling systems established by the relevant culture."* This definition is certainly comprehensive but complicated. Let us try to simplify it. Three conditions must necessarily occur to communicate:

- There must be at least two subjects, one producing and one receiving a message. This exchange can be direct or indirect, as we shall see in a moment.

- There must be a message, something "to be said."

- People must understand the message and thus have a shared code in common. The same language, for example.

Functions of Communication

Communication fulfills several functions. Certainly, it is essential for conveying information because it transforms mental content into words and gestures that allow it to be shared with others. Conversely, it is also useful for learning about the outside world and developing new knowledge. Another fundamental task is to be able to express oneself, providing the image we have of ourselves in terms of values, emotions, status, and social role. In the relationship between the Internet and children, communication assumes a central role of expression, even when practiced online.

Finally, communication is important because it allows us to connect with others and establish satisfying relationships. As social animals, humans need to create and maintain a network of affection that supports them emotionally and practically. In addition, he needs to organize with the community to divide the tasks to be performed and establish rules of coexistence. Good communication skills, therefore, enable him to fulfill these functions best and integrate effectively into society.

Communication Elements

As we have begun to see, communication is made up of several elements that combine to enable exchange among several people.

- **Issuer:** The person who produces the message. He performs an encoding action; that is, he translates his own ideas into a form that the other person can understand.

- **Recipient:** The person who receives the message. He must decode the content he receives, transforming it back into his mental representation. When the audience is large, we speak of public speaking.

- **Message:** The content communicated, the set of information conveyed at the verbal, nonverbal, and paraverbal levels.

- **Code:** How communication is made, the language used. The sender and receiver must share the code for the message to be understood by both.

- **Channel:** The medium through which one communicates. The vocal cords, for example.

- **Context:** The environment within which one communicates. It is given not only to the physical place but also by time, the type of relationship that binds people, the rules of communication, and the cultural aspects of reference. The meaning of communication is closely related to context!

In this way, communication may seem to be a linear phenomenon in which the message passes through a channel from one person to another. In reality, it is correct to speak of a communicative process where the dynamic between sender and receiver is influenced by contextual influences and mutual responses, and feedback. Feedback is a fundamental communication element, clarifying doubts and confirming that the message is understood. It is important because it allows for correcting potential communication errors produced by interference, such as noise or perceptual phenomena, and inaccuracies in the encoding and decoding process. Unclear communication can give rise to conflict.

Channels of Communication

Messages are conveyed through two types of verbal and nonverbal communication, which should be considered sides of the same coin. If someone stops us on the street asking for directions, we are likely to give them verbal instructions accompanied by gestures to indicate the direction to follow. It is because words are always supplemented by body clues that can confirm or deny what is said. However, the reverse is not always true.

Verbal Communication

Verbal communication is nothing but language, the communication mode peculiar to human beings. It is a culturally established system of signs that associates the meaning of a word with its sound. For example, reading the word immediately triggers a connection in our minds that translates into the content we have already stored in our memory. Everyone can interpret it in their own way, referring to trees they have experienced, but they will imagine a prototype built based on common features (a trunk, branches, leaves...).

Nonverbal Communication

Nonverbal communication is present throughout the animal world. It complements content conveyed with language and can sometimes be a communicative form in its own right. For example, think how many meanings a look or a hand gesture can communicate, even if words do not accompany them. Nonverbal communication conveys most of the content (up to 93%) because it provides more information with an emotional impact far greater than language. Nonverbal communication occurs through three different modalities: paralinguistic aspects (or paraverbal communication), i.e., the nonlinguistic cues that personalize one's language, such as tone of voice, rhythm, pauses, or dialect terms; the kinesic realm, i.e., the set of body movements, facial expressions, and gaze; and proxemics, understood as the orientation in space and distance between interlocutors.

Interpersonal and Medial Communication

The easiest communicative exchange to imagine is between two people simultaneously present in the same place. One speaking and the other listening, like two acquaintances greeting each other on the street. This "face-to-face" communication is interpersonal, and contact occurs directly.

Technological development has revolutionized the mode of interaction by introducing the possibility of hearing the message at another time or place than where it was formulated. We are talking about the indirect communication that takes place through the media. A family watching the news from home or a boy receiving a message on his cell phone are not interacting directly with the person who established the initial communicative exchange. The message still arrives, but it follows different rules than traditional communication. First, many more people receive the content produced by one individual.

Moreover, it is possible to choose the content and enjoy it in different spaces and times from those in which it was produced. Consider, for example, the ease with which different television channels or websites can be accessed according to our preferences. Finally, many media communications lack a fundamental element of direct interaction: feedback, the response that transforms monologue into a mutual exchange of content.

Communicative Styles

Communication can be more or less effective depending on the style we adopt during social exchanges. Three basic communicative modes are positioned along a continuum, ranging from aggressiveness to passivity. In between, we find assertiveness, which, as we shall see, is the most functional style. Importantly, styles are behaviors: although people may be predisposed toward one another, their use is variable and depends on the situation. To understand them best, let's look at the different ways of reacting to an event that will have happened to all of us: forgetting to refrigerate the water.

Passive Communication

People who express themselves passively tend to inhibit their emotions and feel embarrassed or anxious during social exchanges. He perceives his own needs as inferior to those of others and does not assert his own positions. Assume the blame for everything wrong. Is afraid of doing wrong, submits without reacting, and avoids conflict. The tone of voice is usually low and insecure.

Answer No. 1: *"I'm terribly sorry, I never get anything right..."*

Active Communication

The energetic style, as opposed to the passive style, is characterized by an excessive imposition of one's own point of view on that of others. It allows one to achieve set goals, but at the expense of the quality of the relationship. There is a perception of being "better," having the right to fabricate, and being hostile and judgmental toward others. So you interrupt the other person and invade his space through aggressive gestures such as the classic "pointing index finger." The interlocutor may come out of the conversation humiliated. This type of communication is also often used in bullying and mobbing incidents.

Answer No. 2: "What a big deal! You always forget to do tons of things, too!"

Assertive Communication

The assertive style is conventionally placed between the first two, although it is a specific communication style. Assertive communication is based on several skills that enable one to feel better about oneself and others. It corresponds to the ability to be able to communicate one's feelings (both positive and negative), to have interpersonal relationships, to express an opinion contrary to that of others, to be able to self-appreciate, but also to recognize one's limitations, to make decisions and exercise choices without excessive anxiety."

Answer No. 3: *"I forgot to refrigerate the water. Is picking up a freshwater bottle at the grocery store okay?"*

A person with an assertive communication style takes an interested and confrontational approach to dialogue. Self-affirmation comes through understanding the other person. There is respect for one's turns of listening and expression, which are taken in a courteous but assertive manner. It is, therefore, an excellent coping strategy!

A key element of this type of communication is resilience, which effectively allows one to overcome "critical" moments in communicative exchanges. Being empathetic also improves communication effectiveness and increases the sense of self-efficacy.

Other skills that one must possess to practice assertive communication, surely the most important ones are:

- Exercising one's own rights and not trampling on those of others.

- Listening to the other person and considering their needs.

- Being honest and truthful.

- Knowing how to recognize one's own emotions to express them correctly.

- Using feedback: giving it and asking for it for good communication clarity.

- Knowing effective ways of managing conflict.

- Not judging and not generalizing.

As we explored in this chapter, communication involves many key components that interact with each other to create meaning and understanding. The way they are used can greatly influence the effectiveness of communication. By mastering the art of communication, we can become better equipped to navigate the challenges of the modern world, from collaborating with colleagues and building meaningful relationships to advocating for ourselves and society. With continued practice and self-reflection, we can develop the communication skills necessary to become effective communicators and, in turn, improve the quality of our interactions with others.

Chapter 4: How to Improve Verbal Communication

Good communication is a cornerstone of our personal and professional life, and it is vital to developing successful relationships, attaining our objectives, and thriving in the world around us. While communication can take various forms, verbal communication is one of the most significant ways we communicate with people. Many of us, however, struggle to express ourselves effectively through spoken words. Perhaps we struggle to express ourselves clearly, or perhaps we struggle to connect with our audience, resulting in misunderstandings and miscommunications.

The good news is that vocal communication is a skill that can be taught and practiced. In this chapter, we'll look at some of the most successful ways to enhance your verbal communication abilities. We'll talk about active listening, body language, speaking clearly and confidently, and establishing a connection with your audience. This chapter will provide you with the tools and strategies you need to take your verbal communication skills to the next level, whether you're a professional looking to improve your workplace communication skills, a student looking to excel in-class presentations, or simply someone who wants to feel more confident and effective in your everyday conversations. So let's dig in and start researching how to become a more confident and effective communicator!

Different Types of Verbal Communication

Words, sounds, and language represent only one part of verbal communication. To communicate effectively with an audience, one must understand who is before you. Based on it, one can divide verbal communication into the following categories:

- Intrapersonal communication: This is the first step to take. One must converse with oneself and express one's ideas. It will give you greater clarity and confidence in your thinking; it will help with decision-making, sentence formation, appropriate words, and effective methods of communicating with others;

- Interpersonal communication: Also known as individual verbal communication, this form occurs between two people. Through it, one can tell whether ideas are being communicated clearly. The other person's reactions, comments, and verbal indicators will help to understand whether what is being communicated is actually being understood;

- Small group communication: Moving from the person to a group of people (team meetings, board meetings, sales meetings, etc.). Because the group is small enough, participants can also converse with each other. Therefore, you need a topic for small group sessions to avoid getting off course. Provide enough time for everyone to talk;

- Public communication: Speaking to a large audience is not easy. This type of communication can include long speeches, political campaigns, presentations, and more. Because the number of participants is larger, you need to use easy-to-understand terms and phrases, perhaps organizing your thoughts before you start speaking.

Paraverbal Communication

Paraverbal communication refers to how we say words, whether we sound happy, sad, angry, determined, etc. Some studies say it accounts for about 30 percent of what we communicate. When a person is angry, for example, they tend to speak faster and in a higher tone. If a person, on the other hand, feels attacked or aggressed, they will respond in short sentences. If a person is bored, he tends to speak slowly and monotonously. Paraverbal communication can also be misinterpreted. Differences such as country of origin and different accents can confuse the listener. For example, certain languages or dialects tend to have higher (or lower) tones regardless of mood. It can confuse those who are not fluent in that language or dialect.

It is important to consider paraverbal communication when expressing yourself. Even if you choose the right words, you may still convey the wrong message if you don't communicate them effectively. So if you want to improve your communication skills, you need to pay more attention, in addition to what you say, to how you say it. Good paraverbal communication gives the words you say more meaning. The same words that you can make noise or inspire.

The Importance of Paraverbal Communication

In addition to having better interpersonal relationships by being able to communicate better (and not be misunderstood), improving your paraverbal communication is especially important for all people who use communication in their work.

For example, you'll need efficient and effective communication whenever you make presentations, promote or launch a new product (or service), in employee training, when communicating changes in the company, and so on.

And if you want to improve in your work and become a leader, you will have to learn how to communicate in the best way possible. Research has shown that presentation style directly impacts a person's perceived charisma. Even if the words are the same, how they are said determines how employees view a leader.

Whether you are making a presentation to important investors or leading a small meeting in your company, you want your listeners to be engaged and interested in the message you want to convey and to see you as a competent person or leader who is confident in what they are saying.

You could spend hours working on the PowerPoint presentation, but how you use preverbal communication will play an important role in how the message is perceived. How you convey your message can increase engagement, arouse emotion, and move the listener to take action. Boost the impact of your message by practicing your paraverbal communication skills.

4 Key Components of Paraverbal Communication

1- Timbre

Voice timbre, also called voice color, refers to how high and low your voice can go. Every person has a particular voice timbre but can change it and make it more lively, enveloping, exciting, deep, and so on. A high timbre can show you are scared, while a lower one can convey calmness and serenity. Timbre can also show authority or anger. Be careful when talking to a child; you will notice that you tend to raise the timbre of your voice to convey happiness and kindness. A high timbre can also communicate nervousness, such as when giving a presentation.

If, on the other hand, we want to convey calmness or communicate something important, we tend to use a lower timbre. Imagine a person saying, "Stay calm," you probably imagined them saying it with a low timbre.

2 - Rhythm

Rhythm means how fast (or slow) you speak. We tend to increase communication speed when nervous or embarrassed (for example, during a presentation). When frightened, we also tend to speak faster. Speaking slower instead shows calmness and being in control of the situation.

In pacing, we can also include pauses. These as well give more meaning to what we say. For example, you can pause after something is said to give it more importance.

3 - Tone

The tone of voice combines factors that can determine or convey meaning. For example, based on the pitch or a different cadence or chant, we can sound sarcastic, angry, happy, sad, serene, and so on.

For example, if you are reading a speech or telling a story, it will sound quite boring if you speak in a monotone tone, while it will be more interesting if you have a more stimulating tone. For example, you can use a stronger emphasis at some points or a faster or slower pace at several points, and soft supporting tones at others. When you vary the tone, you keep the listener more engaged.

The same sentence can have different meanings depending on the tone used. For example, a compliment said in an ironic or sarcastic tone has the intent to hurt instead of praise.

4- Volume

The volume of our voice gives more meaning to what we say and thus is another important aspect of paraverbal communication. If we speak at a high volume, we will give the impression that we are confident people with high self-esteem. Too low a volume, on the other hand, will tend to show shyness and low self-confidence. If you raise your voice too high, you will convey anger, arrogance, and aggression.

How to Improve Your Paraverbal Communication

The tone of voice, loudness, intonation, and pace with which we talk are all examples of paraverbal communication, often known as nonverbal or vocal communication. These factors can impact how others receive and interpret our message, and they play an important part in effective communication. Here are some practical tips to get you started if you want to enhance your paraverbal communication skills:

- Practice active listening: Listening is a vital component of good communication, as well as paraverbal communication. By paying close attention to what the other person is saying, you show that you value your time together. As a result, you will be able to develop a more upbeat and engaging tone of voice.
- Pay attention to your tone: Your voice expresses your emotions, attitudes, and intentions. Focus on employing a warm, welcoming tone when appropriate to strengthen your paraverbal communication. Avoid using a monotone or condescending tone of voice, as this can turn people off and impede efficient communication.
- Vary your pace: The rate at which you talk greatly impacts how your message is received. Speaking too quickly can cause

people to lose attention while speaking too slowly can cause them to lose interest. Adapt your pace to the situation and audience.

- Use inflection to convey meaning: Inflection is the rise and fall of your speaking voice. Using inflection, you can accentuate particular words and phrases and add significance and depth to your message. Try various inflections to determine which ones work best for you.

- Monitor your volume: Others may find hearing and comprehending you difficult if you speak too loudly or softly. Strive to speak at a moderate volume that is comfortable for both you and your audience to increase your paraverbal communication.

- Be mindful of your body language: Your body language can also impact paraverbal communication. When speaking, try to maintain an open posture, with your arms and legs uncrossed, and make eye contact with your audience. It will help convey that you're approachable, engaged, and confident.

It takes time and practice to improve your paraverbal communication abilities, but by adopting these strategies into your regular talks and interactions, you may establish a more successful and engaging communication style. Mastering the art of paraverbal communication can help you achieve your goals and connect more deeply with people, whether you're a business professional, educator, or simply someone trying to better your relationships.

How to Master Small Talk

Want to discover the secrets of effective communication? You don't need a course, exercises made in the 1990s, or fancy techniques. Here are simple tricks to improve any conversation in less than 5 minutes (time to read this section).

Communication plays a critical role in the success of our relationships. *Not convinced of that? Try to think about it-who do you love to spend time with? Who do you like best among your friends? Who would you invite to your wedding even if they are not your third cousin?* Yep, the people we love to converse with are also the people with whom we have the most affinity. After that, a question arises--are you also one of these people with whom it is pleasant to converse? No? Let me guess...

- When you find yourself in a conversation, especially with a person you've met for the first time (or know little about yet), you feel awkward and don't quite know what to talk about.

- After the ritual questions, awkward silences often follow between you and your interlocutor.

- You often feel that your conversations remain on the surface, and you have difficulty really connecting with people.

If you have found yourself in one of these situations at least once, let's discover together some effective communication techniques that can dramatically improve your conversations. But first, some brief background.

Effective communication is assessed by the ability to make the interlocutor perceive the exact meaning of the message one wants to convey crystal-clearly without the slightest danger of being misunderstood. Effective communication, therefore, means expressing oneself to the best of one's ability and establishing satisfying relationships with which one can share needs, values, and goals. Improving communication, therefore, allows one to get in tune with one's interlocutors, to listen actively, and to respect those in front of us with the possibility of inward enrichment.

Learn to Ask Questions (The Right Ones)

Questions are one of the most powerful communication tools at our disposal. Asking the right questions can change our lives. Asking the right questions can change the quality of our conversations. So let's see what the best questions you can ask during a chat to connect with your interlocutor immediately are. Okay, I'd say we've been around this long enough; I certainly don't want to lose you in this... "long-distance conversation." Here are the 9 tools that will forever improve your conversations by giving you a big hand in getting closer and closer to effective communication:

1. Stop interrogating

Effective communication with others is, first and foremost, "rich" communication. If you force your interlocutor (the girl/boyfriend you've fallen in love with, the customer you'd like to win over, the acquaintance you'd like to know more about) to answer in monosyllables, believe me, your conversation won't get very far!

"Dry" questions that involve a "yes/no" response can be a good icebreaker, but if you keep asking these questions, perhaps even at a rapid pace, you will put the other person on the defensive, and your communication will suffer. Instead, choose open questions that allow the other person to open up (precisely) and engage in a real dialogue with you.

Example: Don't ask, "Do you like music?" Instead, ask, "Which artist do you like? Why this particular artist?"

2. Use "Why?" (at least 3 times)

When I was a child, my parents once gave me a book called "Why? Why?": I must have been a real first-class pain in the ass! Yet that simple word, "Why," can improve our conversations. If you don't want to limit yourself to superficial chit-chat and want to go deep with the person in front of you, show sincere curiosity: ask why they answer.

Example: if your interlocutor tells you that he loves Justin Bieber because of his song lyrics, ask him, "Why do you love his lyrics? What are some passages you particularly love?" if he replies that he is attached to a particular passage, asking him "Why?" (in a curious, non-pushy way) is one of the best ways to deepen a conversation.

3. Ask precise questions

Specific questions lead the interlocutor to give rich and detailed answers. The next time you see a colleague after the weekend, don't ask him how the weekend went; ask him what the most fun activity he did was.

Again, if you apply the advice in this section in a mechanical and forced way, you will make your conversations very awkward. Instead, take a cue from these tips to naturally improve your effective communication skills.

Talk about emotions and reactions

If you talk to someone about their work or passion, don't ask them generic questions like, *"What is it like to be a lawyer?"* These are general questions and are difficult to answer. Instead, focus on the person's emotions and reactions - *"what is the one thing that has amazed you the most since you have been a lawyer?"*, *"What is one thing you never expected before you embarked on a medical career?"*

Speak to people's hearts, don't put them on the spot with bland questions.

Be always curious

Often conversations between people rather than an engaging exchange resemble a competition in which each interlocutor spends time waiting for their turn, thinking of something clever and brilliant to say, and effectively ignoring what the others are saying. Many people do this, but trust me: it is noticeable.

Instead, learn to be curious: listen to the answer with sincere attention after asking a question. You will be surprised at how many new things you can discover, which will raise new questions, making the conversation fun and never boring.

... and then remember, as Dale Carnegie said: *people love to talk about themselves; the more you make them do it, the more they will love you.*

Learn lessons from other people

Effective communication is two-way communication. In the previous points, we have seen how to use questions to put your interlocutor at ease and have an engaging and deep conversation. But these conversations must enrich you as well. Otherwise, the risk is that they become a communication game for their own sake.

One of the best ways to spark the conversation and glean as many secrets as possible from a particularly stimulating interlocutor is to ask that person what lessons they have learned from a given circumstance or experience.

Often we are so self-centered that we forget that other people have probably already faced similar challenges to ours, and their experience can teach us a lot: just ask what lessons they have learned.

Let me tell you a story

Human beings live by stories. Since ancient times, stories have been our favorite communicative tool for conveying knowledge. If you want an interesting conversation, give your interlocutor a chance to tell you a story.

If you are talking to a guy or girl you like, don't just ask him or her what he or she does for a living; rather, ask him or her to tell you the craziest thing that has happened to him or her since he or she has been working. Telling stories is as natural as it gets for any human being: doing so puts us at ease and creates empathy with the people we are conversing with.

Take a cue from the children

A few paragraphs ago, I told you what a pain-in-the-ass child I was as a child with all my "Why? Why?" but children could teach us something else. Children are not afraid to ask (seemingly) stupid questions.

On the other hand, we adults are always jerking our heads, and if our interlocutor says something we don't understand, we sketch a smile and move on bad mistake! If you don't understand something, simply ask the person in front of you to explain it to you again, perhaps as you would explain it to a 4-year-old child.

Use this bonus question

If you find yourself talking to an expert and want to get the most out of the conversation, you should definitely use this bonus question:

"What is the question that no one ever asks you that you think is critical to success in your field?"

This question will make your interlocutor feel important, but more importantly, it will open up a world for you! Many of us are convinced that we already know everything about a topic, but when we offer a point of view that we had never thought of and were totally unaware of, we really expand our knowledge. Let the duty expert find the most intelligent questions they want to answer.

Mastering small talk is a talent that can help you in various situations, from professional networking to social connections. You can develop new connections, strengthen relationships, and improve your general social and emotional intelligence by learning to begin and engage in conversations easily.

To master small conversation, remember that it's not simply about exchanging pleasantries or making small talk about making small talk. Small chat allows you to connect with people on a deeper level, learn about their interests and opinions, and establish common ground. In the long run, you can make more significant connections by carefully listening, displaying real interest, and being authentic in your communication. In addition to these critical methods, practicing and being patient with yourself is critical. Mastering small talk, like any talent, requires time and effort, but with practice, it will become easier and more natural. Remember to stay present in the moment, be careful of your body language, and take an active interest in the individuals you're conversing with.

To summarize, a small chat may appear insignificant, but it is important for developing relationships and connecting with others. You may boost your confidence, broaden your social circle, and enrich your personal and professional life by mastering the art of small conversation. Now, apply these tactics to begin mastering the art of small conversation immediately!

How to Cope With Different Situations

Adapting your communication style to varied contexts and audiences is an important part of this. In this section, we'll look at some practical advice and tactics for modifying your communication style in various situations.

Adapting to Different Gender Styles

Men and women often communicate in different ways, and adjusting to these differences can help you develop better connections and avoid misunderstandings. Males tend to use more direct language and focus more on facts and outcomes, whereas women tend to use more indirect language and prioritize connection-building. It is critical to be aware of these distinctions and change your approach when adapting your communication style to different genders. Be aware of your language, tone, and body language, and try to match the communication style of the person you are conversing with.

Adapting to Public Speaking

Public speaking can be intimidating, but you can deliver an interesting and powerful presentation with proper preparation and strategy. One key to success is adapting your communication style to the audience and situation. Be precise and concise, utilizing proper tone and tempo, and engage your audience with examples and tales. Body language and eye contact are vital for connecting with your audience and conveying confidence and power.

Adapting to Different Levels of Formality

Depending on the situation and audience, the level of formality in a communication setting can vary greatly. Speaking with colleagues, for example, may be more casual than interacting with clients or superiors. Pay attention to the tone and language used in the communication context, and alter your language and body language accordingly, to adapt your communication style to varied levels of formality. Be respectful, but also aim to establish a connection with your audience by being warm and approachable.

Adapting to Cross-Cultural Communication

Cross-cultural communication might be difficult, but it also provides an opportunity to learn and interact with people from various backgrounds. It is critical to be conscious of cultural differences in communication styles, body language, and nonverbal clues while adapting your communication style to different cultures. Be respectful and open-minded, and try to learn about the individuals you're engaging with's cultural norms and communication patterns.

Adapting to Social vs. Professional Contexts

The level of formality and tone of the communication might also differ based on whether you're conversing in a social or professional setting. Be aware of the right tone and vocabulary for each situation while adapting your communication style to different contexts. In a social setting, more informal language and humor may be suitable, yet a more formal and straightforward communication style may be more appropriate in a professional setting.

Changing your communication style to various contexts and audiences is an important ability for effective communication. You may connect more successfully with others, develop deeper connections, and achieve your goals by being attentive to the specific context and audience and modifying your vocabulary, tone, and body language accordingly. With practice and commitment, anyone can learn to alter their communication style and become a more effective communicator.

Exercises to Improve Your Communication

This chapter will introduce you to several strategies for enhancing your verbal communication abilities through practice and exploration. These drills will help you become a more confident and persuasive speaker, whether your goal is to give better speeches in front of large audiences, have deeper conversations with friends and family, or simply speak up more.

To perfect your spoken language, try these exercises, which range from using a voice recorder to monitor your speech to reading aloud to improve your pronunciation and clarity to active listening and visualization techniques. So, let's dive in and check out all the ways you can improve your communication skills to the point where you can easily persuade others.

Use a Voice Recorder to Monitor Your Speech

Having a recording of your own voice can help you figure out what you can do to become a better communicator. By listening to your recorded voice, you can analyze your tone, inflection, pacing, and other aspects of your speech that might be hindering effective communication. You can also practice reading articles, speeches, or other texts aloud and listen back to identify areas that need improvement.

Expand Your Conversation Topics

One of the best ways to improve your verbal communication skills is by practicing conversation skills with unfamiliar people. Try to strike up conversations with people you meet throughout the day, such as cashiers, baristas, or coworkers you don't know well. Try to expand your conversation topics and engage in active listening to show your interest and build rapport.

Read Aloud to Improve Pronunciation and Clarity

Reading aloud is an excellent way to improve your pronunciation and clarity of speech. Try reading articles, books, or other texts aloud, focusing on enunciating each word clearly and with proper intonation. You can also record yourself reading aloud and listen back to identify areas for improvement.

Practice Speaking with Confidence

The ability to speak with assurance is essential in any professional setting. Practice making your voice heard by a mirror or a close friend or relative to boost your self-confidence. Focus on maintaining good posture, eye contact, and speaking clearly and with conviction. Remember to take deep breaths and speak steadily to help control any nervousness.

Join a Public Speaking Group or Take a Class

Public speaking groups or classes can be an excellent way to improve your verbal communication skills in a supportive and constructive environment. These groups typically offer opportunities to practice speaking in front of an audience, receive feedback, and learn from other speakers. Some popular public speaking groups include Toastmasters and Public Speaking Academy.

In conclusion, verbal communication is a critical skill that can benefit you in all areas of your life. Incorporating these exercises and techniques into your daily routine can improve your verbal communication skills and help you achieve your goals. Remember to practice regularly, stay positive, and be patient with yourself. With time and effort, anyone can become a more confident and effective communicator.

Chapter 5: Assertive Communication

We all communicate all the time, every day in private life and the workplace. Yet few people have ever stopped to think seriously about how they communicate. Assertiveness is concerned with giving a map describing the various ways people communicate. It also provides the tools for developing assertive communication.

In this chapter, we will first see what is meant by 'assertive communication' and what irrational ideas make us think unassertively. Then I will give you some tips that you can put into practice from today to communicate assertively.

What Is Assertive Communication?

Giving an actual definition of assertive communication might be reductive and ineffective compared to describing the phenomenon as something broader and decidedly less tied to strict terminology. Assertive communication is an attitude of the employer, the employee, and, more simply, of people, which denotes a certain ability to transmit concepts, and thoughts clearly and directly.

Assertive communication is that characteristic whereby a person can assert, that is, to assert with the certainty that it is true, to claim as certain something. Although we can trace an assertive style to this verb, it is, as mentioned, a concept whose meaning is broader. In general, assertiveness is the ability to be confident and to appear so, but without being aggressive.

In an assertive climate, a person can make a confident statement or affirm a statement without the need for proof. To be assertive is to speak up for what you believe in and your rights clearly, honestly, and respectfully.

What Assertive Communication Consists of

Assertiveness is an important aspect of communication abilities. Being assertive means being able to communicate and assert oneself while respecting the ideas and rights of others. Assertive communication is founded on mutual respect and is both effective and diplomatic. Being assertive demonstrates that you value yourself because you are ready to defend your interests and express your thoughts and feelings.

It also demonstrates that you know others' rights and needs and are ready to work actively to resolve conflicts. It is also why assertive behavior boosts your self-esteem and gets others' respect. If you are someone who cannot say no, learning to be assertive will help you deal with many circumstances that cause stress and discomfort. Some individuals appear to have an innate tendency to be assertive, but for most of us, assertiveness is a talent that can be learned. Of course, not only what you say in words matters, but also how you express it. Assertive communication is direct and respectful. It improves the chances of getting a message across and for it to be considered. Assertiveness consists of the following:

- Recognizing and expressing one's emotions
- Standing up for one's rights
- Manifesting one's needs, preferences, desires, criticisms

In a manner:

- Honest

- Direct

- Appropriate

- Respecting the rights and not the desires of others

An example of assertive communication may be trivially saying 'I don't like him' instead of 'he is bad' or 'you can't cook.' Learning to communicate assertively does not guarantee that you will get what you want but will make it much more likely. It will also improve your relationships with other people.

What you say does not have to be said just for others who may not even agree with you. The goal must not be to convince others. You have to do it for yourself to show that you can respond and are your master. Good self-esteem is the basis of assertiveness, and communicating improves self-esteem assertively.

How to Communicate Assertively

Use 'I' statements, and be clear and forthright:

- 'I would appreciate it if you could repay me.'

- 'I think what you have done is good, but I would like you to...'

Describe how the other person's conduct makes you feel; doing so alerts people to the consequences of their actions:

- 'You scare me when you elevate your voice... I'd like you to talk more quietly.'

- 'You confound me when you don't tell me how you feel about it.'

Hold your ground - use the broken record technique. Doing so entails deciding upon an approach, formulating a statement, and restating it for as long as is required:

- *'I would appreciate it if you could reimburse me... Yes, but I still want my money back... I understand what you're saying, but I still want my money back.'*

The What & The How

Communication consists of both what you say, that is, the words that come out of your mouth. What part of the message could you write on paper, and would it still stay the same? If applied without a fair amount of practice and an understanding of their ideas, many assertiveness techniques lead to working only at this level. To assertively communicate, you'd better prepare what to say first and practice the tips from before. For what to say when you have to handle others' aggression, there are defensive techniques that explain what you should say.

For example, saying 'don't get angry' usually only does damage during an argument. Telling a person 'don't get angry' is manipulative. It is me ordering you to change your emotions because I feel attacked or otherwise annoyed by y our expression of anger.

Simply put, I am telling a person I can see who cannot control their emotions to control them because I cannot handle the effect they have on me. A simple advice is to speak in the first person about what you think and see. I can at most ask, assertively, 'you seem to be angry, is something bothering you?'

The way instead is represented by nonverbal language, so by facial expression, gestures, tone of voice, etc. Nonverbal language also conveys a message with the difference that it is more difficult to control and be aware of. Most people give more weight to nonverbal communication of the message and how it differs. You may have heard yourself say 'thank you' but perceive it as a 'f*ck you.'

If you want your communication to be truly assertive, you must also work on how that is your nonverbal behavior. It helps you a lot to try not to react emotionally to what people say to us. Otherwise, the risk is ending up arguing. The same words said in two different tones, different facial expressions, and different postures will have two different results in others. It is because you are communicating different messages with your nonverbal communication.

An example is sarcasm. If you take sarcasm literally, it has the opposite meaning.

To work on how you communicate your words, there is a secret: practice! You can help yourself by rehearsing with people you are familiar with or recording what you say.

Thinking Assertively

We are what we think. You need to have assertive ideas in your head and not act them out to communicate assertively. It, therefore, becomes essential to think assertively. It is precisely thoughts and beliefs that determine emotions and behavior. If, for example, someone parks in front of your garage, you know that the parking ban protects you. If you have to assert yourself with the car owner, you know you are right. The law is on your side. That is why it is important to understand the theoretical concepts of assertiveness.

You need to know your assertive rights, which are the laws of assertiveness. They give you confidence when you have to assert yourself and clarify what you can ask for and what you can demand. In the same way, however, you must recognize the same rights as others.

Above all, you have to understand -- and give yourself time to 'digest' -- that you have the right to communicate assertively. It is the basis, though. You cannot hope that just thinking will make you assertive. If you start practicing, you will also find that your attitude and behavior will change how you think and feel.

Start paying attention to how you talk to yourself. You can do nothing to prevent certain thoughts from going through your mind, but you can begin to cultivate a positive and assertive way of talking to yourself. Try to identify your automatic thoughts. Automatic thoughts are the first ones that go through your mind when you are uncomfortable. Once you identify them, try to respond positively and realistically. Try to notice when they come to your mind, 'here are my unassertive thoughts.' Keeping a journal where you write and question them helps a lot.

IRRATIONAL IDEAS

Irrational ideas and assertive rights are part of assertiveness's belief map. The cognitive level deals with the thoughts and beliefs we have learned from our experiences and the conditioning of the culture in which we live. Albert Ellis' Irrational Ideas:

- I must always be loved, approved, and esteemed by all the people significant to me.

- I must always show myself competent and adequate in everything I do.

- Things must go so that I can get everything I want immediately and effortlessly; otherwise, the world sucks, and life is not worth living.

- Others must treat everyone fairly: if they behave unfairly or immorally, they are rotters and deserve to be severely punished. They must serve it one way or another.

- If I fear that something dangerous or harmful might happen, then I have to think about it all the time, and it is right that I should be agitated at the thought of possible consequences so that I can control them better.

- I must find perfect solutions to my own problems or those of others; otherwise, who knows what may happen!

- The cause of my emotions and feelings is always external, so there is little I can do to control them to overcome depression and anxiety. Resentment.

- My past is the real cause of my current problems: if anything has heavily affected my life. It irretrievably affects all my current feelings and behavior.

- I need to be quiet, without responsibility, effort, discipline, or self-control.

- I must always be perfectly comfortable and without suffering of any kind.

- I could go crazy, and that would be really terrible.

- I consider myself weak, incapable, and inadequate. So I need to depend on others and someone in particular.

- Which of these irrational ideas is part of your beliefs?

Smart Tips for Communicating Assertively

- When you expound your ideas, don't burden others, don't make them feel guilty, but clarify what you prefer.

- Pay attention to the sense of obligation when you feel you have to do something. Always ask yourself if it makes sense.

- The criteria you use to evaluate yourself and others should not be rigid but elastic. Circumstances must be taken into account.

- You get absorbed in those mechanisms if you stay within a particular environment or group.

- Do not judge. You can only observe others' behavior and try to understand it instead of judging it.

- Don't pretend to teach others how to communicate; if you're good, you must manage them. Those who are unassertive need people to communicate with them assertively.

- No one is perfect! We all say something wrong from time to time.

- Experience is very important in learning to communicate assertively and cannot be avoided.

- The right recipe comes from having good ingredients in the right quantity and working well. Two memorized phrases are not enough, and working only on the verbal part is not enough.

Assertive Communication: Examples

In response to a friend's invitation to accompany him to the opera:

- 'No thanks. I appreciate your offer and thank you for considering me, but I don't like the opera.'

- I am not completely satisfied with the situation. Could you propose some other solution?

In response to the boss criticizing an employee's work: 'The work you did is no good. We've lost money; we can't go on like this.'

- 'I understand your frustration, and I'm sorry; that was not my intention. I thought my work was in line with what you requested, though, and I struggled to see my mistake. To avoid going on like this, I would be pleased to set some goals and tasks in black and white with her so that I can confidently devote myself to what she deems most productive.

To a colleague who does not respond to emails and does not hear back:

- 'I've sent you three emails and haven't heard back. I guess you have been busy and are not doing this on purpose. However, I need your report in time to draft the year-end report for the 15th. From the 10th I will be away on business and cannot devote myself to this activity as I have already anticipated to our boss and you. Your material is the only one I am missing; everyone delivered it to me last week, and I honestly wanted to finish it all this week. When do you think you can get it to me?'

Chapter 6: How to Become a Skilled Communicator

What you say is less significant than how you say it. That picture is so sad, but it's the truth. More often than not, how you say something alters its intended meaning. My immediate environment, including my home and workplace, was thoroughly examined. Those who can convey their ideas to others effectively are more likely to succeed in their endeavors, whether a company employs them, run a traditional business, or are self-employed.

Successfully interacting with others is necessary in the modern world, and communicating effectively is crucial. I want to describe my steps to develop my skills in this field. As a young adult, I believed that nobody likes a chatty person. I learned from my mistake much later in life.

The world depends on verbal exchanges for survival. There are many channels through which ideas can be conveyed, but the most immediate is verbal exchange. It's the hardest to master, in my opinion. *I mean, when you really want to tell someone, "Go to h***," how do you say it without sounding so harsh?* This chapter will explore additional strategies for improving your communication skills.

How to Make a Great First Impression

I think it's important to be genuine when we meet new people, but I also recognize the role that sublimation can play. First impressions are formed not only by the words we use but also by our body language, tone of voice, eye contact, etc.

For better communication with others, whether in a professional setting (such as when networking) or a social one (such as when talking to a cute guy or girl), I have compiled a list of five simple tips that can help.

1. Show some genuine curiosity

Everyone you meet is living a story worth telling; the best way to learn that story is to genuinely care about what the other person is going through.

Human intuition is just pattern recognition, which can be helpful in certain circumstances but isn't always accurate. If you want to really understand what someone is saying to you, you should actively engage in active listening. Determine what they mean by their words by applying your best judgment.

2. Always give genuine compliments

People can look beyond superficial characteristics, so when you compliment, focus on the person's actions rather than their genetic make-up. It's a deeper route to take. So, when you feel the urge to lavish praise on someone, ensure it comes from a place of sincerity.

3. Allow yourself to be helped and advised

When we help others, we feel good about ourselves, and the brain learns to value the other person's contribution. Franklin recognized the brain's natural tendency to seek congruence between behavior and thought, and he frequently borrowed literature and other resources from his political opponents to win them over. The Franklin effect describes this phenomenon.

4. A good mental outlook

The key to a successful first impression is a confident demeanor. A bad attitude will always shine through, regardless of how well you dress or groom yourself.

It's not always easy to put forward a positive attitude, especially in stressful situations like an interview where you're likely nervous. Putting in the effort to listen carefully and look them in the eye sends a message of interest and respect, which can help you establish rapport and credibility.

5. Make direct eye contact

Making initial contact through eye contact is essential. It isn't nice to look around the room as if you're trying to find a better conversation partner. Looking down at the ground makes you appear insecure while looking up and down someone else's body can come across as condescending. Maintaining a healthy level of eye contact is essential, but you shouldn't stare intently at the other person either.

People who see intelligence in your eyes will like you no matter how you look.

How to Ice Break

It's not easy to start a conversation with someone you've just met or doesn't know very well, but doing so is crucial for making new friends and expanding your social circle. If you're in a professional or social setting and need to start a conversation with someone new, you might feel nervous or unsure what to say. However, mastering the art of breaking the ice can help you make a favorable impression on others, leading to the development of personal and professional relationships.

Finding a common interest, asking a question with an open-ended response, using humor, demonstrating empathy, and using the right body language are all great ways to start conversations with new people. These methods can help you strike up a conversation with someone in a way that makes them feel comfortable and at ease.

Discovering a shared interest is a great way to break the ice and start a conversation with a new person. Finding common ground through shared experiences or hobbies is an excellent way to break the ice and open the door to a more in-depth discussion. Using open-ended questions is also important in maintaining a lively and interesting conversation. With your help, the other person will feel more comfortable talking about themselves and their interests, strengthening your bond with them.

Making people laugh is a great way to get them to open up and feel comfortable around you. Keep your sense of humor in check, and don't let the other person feel offended, though. The ability to empathize with the other person is also crucial. When you show the other person that you've heard them and care about what they have to say, you earn their trust and respect.

Finally, using the right body language is essential for breaking the ice. Make yourself more approachable, interested, and engaged by using open body language, eye contact, and mirroring the other person's body language.

How to Keep Conversation Going

One of the most important aspects of effective communication is keeping the conversation going even when it appears to be losing steam. In this chapter, we'll look at some practical tips and strategies for keeping the conversation flowing naturally and keeping your conversational partner engaged.

Clearly and briefly express yourself

One of the most vital skills in maintaining a conversation is expressing oneself clearly and concisely. It entails taking the time to consider what you want to say before saying it and using simple language. Consider the following when doing so:

- Avoid using jargon or technical terms that your conversation partner may not understand.

- Stay on topic and avoid abruptly switching from one topic to another.

- Avoid long-winded explanations or stories that may lose your listener's attention by being direct and to the point.

- Use active listening skills to ensure that you are heard and understood,

- Avoid monopolizing the discussion.

Another important aspect of keeping the conversation going is to avoid monopolizing it. Allowing your conversational partner to contribute to the conversation and share their thoughts and opinions is critical. Consider the following to avoid dominating the conversation:

- Take turns speaking and actively listening to what your conversation partner is saying.

- Interrupting or talking over your conversation partner can be seen as rude or disrespectful.

- Ask open-ended questions to encourage your conversation partner to share their thoughts and opinions.

- Encourage your conversation partner to continue speaking using nonverbal cues such as nodding or smiling.

Request Opinions and Points of View

Asking for your conversational partner's opinions and points of view is one of the most effective ways to keep the conversation going. It not only demonstrates your appreciation for their input, but it can also lead to more interesting and engaging conversations. Consider the following when soliciting opinions and viewpoints:

- Ask open-ended questions to encourage your conversation partner to share their thoughts and opinions.

- Avoid asking leading questions that imply an answer or point of view.

- Be genuinely interested in your conversation partner's point of view and actively listen to what they say.

- Even if you disagree with your conversation partner's opinions and views, respond to them respectfully and constructively.

- Use icebreakers and conversation starters.

If you're having trouble keeping the conversation going, using conversation starters and icebreakers can be beneficial. These are simple, open-ended questions or statements that can help to restart the conversation. Conversation starters and icebreakers include the following:

- "What do you enjoy doing for fun?"

- "Tell me about your most memorable vacation."

- "Can you tell me about something interesting you recently learned?"

- "Do you have any animals? Please tell me about them."

You can keep the conversation going and build stronger connections with your conversational partner by using these conversation starters and icebreakers.

All the Secrets of Non-Verbal Communication

Understanding nonverbal communication and the meaning of gestures is the first step in learning how to read other people's body language and control the messages you unwittingly send through nonverbal communication.

Knowing how to read body language and communicate with gestures and posture is a great advantage in professional situations, such as sales, or in any context where you have to persuade someone and bargain. It can be decisive at critical moments.

Having exercises and examples of nonverbal communication enables you to train yourself and read the situation on the fly when you are stressed and have other things on your mind. With training, you will be able to recognize the subtle differences between people and avoid making hasty assumptions such as "if a person crosses his arms, he is protective."

How to Read Body Language

Nonverbal communication should always be interpreted in the environment in which it occurs. First and foremost, in the context of the person you are dealing with. Everyone has a behavioral foundation that must be established before any conclusions can be drawn. Some individuals, for example, are naturally nervous, such calming movements like rubbing their fingers or biting their lips may be ineffective. Even the smallest calming gesture can mean a lot to someone who is usually calm and composed.

People cross their arms for a variety of reasons: they are defensive, tired, cold, or have something on their thoughts that has nothing to do with you, or they simply do it out of habit. A gesture can signify anything and everything. It must first be considered in the individual and situation context.

Practice Nonverbal Positive Communication

How we approach others with nonverbal communication, which is often unconscious, conveys a clear message to those around us. Establishing a positive statement in our actions can significantly, even if silent, impact our success.

Start your day by devoting 10 minutes to listing three items you are grateful for. Then consider three goals you want to achieve. Consider and recall three powerful emotions connected with those objectives. For example, today is your first appointment with an important client, and you want it to go well. You want to experience and express contentment, confidence, and determination.

So, walk with purpose and a genuine smile on your face. Straighten your back and look forwards. Always walk with assurance and a smile. Your body interacts with you as well as with others. Emotions affect the stance, and posture affects emotions. If you can invigorate yourself with your body language, it will also work on others!

Examples of Body Gestures and Their Application

- Here are some exercises in silent communication:

- Stand tall and place your hands behind your back. Inhale power and self-assurance. The response of another individual is the kind of deference you show to a general.

- Raise your arms in a V configuration. The victory gives you power, confidence, and exhilaration.

- It is not a gesture you would usually make in front of others, but it can help you control your emotions and attitude.

- Open your limbs. Satisfaction and joy at something positive that has occurred. Take in admiration and acclaim.

- Put your hands on your shoulders. Dominance. Show confidence and respect.

- Open your shoulders and your ankles. Confidence, dominance, and being prepared to move. Encourages others to believe in your talents.

- Take a breath. Authority and power. Instill respect.

- Straight back. Self-assurance, power, dominance, competence, and pride. Instills confidence and respect in your skills.

Exercises In Reading Others' Nonverbal Communication

When you are emotionally engaged, it is more difficult to interpret people's nonverbal communication. If, on the other hand, you watch situations in which you have no particular interest, you will be more objective, which is necessary for practicing reading body language.

- Go to a public location, bar, or shopping mall and:

- Consider how a person's gender and cultural background influence their bodily expressions.

- Examine the various body movements and facial expressions. Do they go together? What emotions do they show?

Visit locations where you can see two individuals interacting with each other.

- Do they imitate each other's facial gestures, indicating that they like each other?

- Look for barriers and evidence of separation. Perhaps one person moves back in a chair or places an object between himself and the other to indicate that he is unsure and does not want to offer more assurance.

- Observe one person's gestures, try to figure out what they mean, and then watch the other person's response. What are the two individuals saying?

Exercises on People You Know'S Body Language

Consider ten individuals you've worked with.

- How would you characterize their behavior and presentation? Rigid, relaxed, or careless? Did their looks correspond to their demeanor?

- What could you have done differently with each of them to influence their conduct more effectively? How could you turn up and act differently to gain a stronger grip on them?

Try to detect signs of stress during business meetings with coworkers, who are typically more honest about their emotions than clients.

- Make a mental note of every nonverbal communication and gesture and what you believe it means.

- Make a list of which gestures a person uses regularly and which ones indicate something particular, such as stress or discomfort.

- Mute the sound while watching a performance or a television series. Try to deduce what is going on from the characters' movements. If the character's gestures and facial expressions are inconsistent, you're either dealing with a bad actor or the character isn't genuine.

Verbal Communication'S Subtext

You can study the purpose behind lines of dialogue by watching movies and television shows. When one individual interacts with another to elicit a response, they do the following:

- By posing a straightforward query.

- By providing a reward.

- By using an emotional plea.

- By utilizing the ego.

- By assisting the other individual in overcoming fear.

- By instilling certainty or uncertainty in the mind of the other individual.

- Silence is being used to occupy a vacuum.

Take note of how one person's purpose causes the other person to react.

- Examine politicians, ambassadors, and others who have received media training.

- Is the person providing direct answers or evasive ones?

- What do you notice in a person's body language when they avoid answering a question? Changes in tone of voice, speech rhythm, or stress indications should be noted.

Under certain conditions, some people speak without subtext, saying what they precisely think. However, it is not uncommon for a hidden meaning beneath the surface of the words that is implied in the consequences of the words.

Exercises in Gestures

Seek out individuals you can trust to point out your body language. What are your typical hand gestures? How would you behave in a hypothetical situation? Then observe how your nonverbal language changes in response to your feelings.

- How do you show your rage? What is your body language from head to toe, from the moment you are irritated to the moment you are furious?

- When you're anxious, how do you show it? Consider not only your movements but also your nonverbal energy levels.

- When you are defensive, how does your conduct change? Do you have a hunched back? Do you get up from behind your desk? Do you have your wrists crossed?

The more precise you can analyze your gestures, the more control you will have when the time comes. We often know our feelings, which are still expressed through our bodies. We can better comprehend ourselves by observing ourselves.

Implementing Stress Reactions in Nonverbal Communication

Nonverbal communication relies heavily on stress reactions. We define stress as any circumstance that causes discomfort, not work-related stress.

People typically express their stress in their own unique manner. When you walk into an office, sit down for an important meeting, or talk in front of an audience, your body automatically vents your stress with a sequence of calming gestures intended to make you feel better.

Some people nibble their fingers, and others rub one foot against the other. Still, others grin, turn their smartphones back in their fingers, and so on.

Remember that every gesture has a different meaning depending on the individual. Before you can interpret it, you must first understand how that individual normally behaves, and if something deviates from normal, you must consider why. Perhaps that person is nervous not because of what you said but because they had a dispute with their son the day before. Everything is dependent on context.

Nonverbal communication has a diverse and subtle lexicon that can be classified into several meaning categories:

- Gestures are used to highlight words and stress their significance. As an example, pointing a pointer.

- Gestures are designed to convey something. They enhance the meaning of words or give them a more exact nuance. Nodding, for example, encourages the other individual to continue speaking.

- Gestures are used to relieve tension and discomfort. For example, fidgeting with one's earrings or biting one's nails.

- Gestures are used to form a barrier to protect oneself or to indicate distance. From crossing your arms to physically placing an item in front of you, there are many ways to express yourself.

Keep this in mind as you observe people in your daily existence. Always think about what this individual is really saying. What is the intention that you may not be conscious of?

On a conscious level, you will also observe micro gestures that are almost invisible. They are small eye expressions, tensions, and glances that appear and vanish in milliseconds. They are nothing more than thoughts that appear for a brief moment in the physical universe of the body.

How to Improve Your Non-Verbal Communication

Effective communication relies heavily on nonverbal cues. It refers to the messages we send to our bodies, facial expressions, and other nonverbal cues. In this chapter, we'll look at practical tips and strategies for improving nonverbal communication, including manual gestures, posture, eyes, lips, and feet.

Hand Gestures

The hand movements we use to convey meaning and emphasize our words are manual gestures. Using appropriate manual gestures can help improve your message's engagement and persuasiveness.

Consider the following suggestions to help you improve your manual gestures:

- Make hand gestures that correspond to the content of your message. For example, if you're describing something circular, you could make a circular gesture with your hands.

- Tap your fingers or play with your hair to avoid making repetitive or distracting gestures.

- Use your hands to highlight important points or make your message more interesting and engaging.

- When using manual gestures, remember cultural differences, as different cultures may have different meanings for the same gesture.

Posture

Posture refers to how we hold our bodies, which can reveal much about our confidence and authority. Poor posture can make you appear uninterested or disengaged, whereas good posture can help you appear more confident and engaged. Consider the following suggestions for bettering your posture:

- Straighten your back, shoulders back, and chest open.

- Cross your arms or slouch to signal that you're closed off and defensive.

- Make eye contact with your conversation partner to demonstrate that you're engaged and interested in what they're saying.

- Avoid fidgeting or shifting your weight from one foot to the other, as these behaviors can distract or convey nervousness.

Eyes

It's said that a person's eyes are the "windows to the soul" because they reveal a great deal about their true feelings and motivations. Avoiding eye contact can make you appear untrustworthy or dishonest, whereas making eye contact can make you appear more confident and trustworthy. To make better use of your gaze, consider the following tips:

- To show that you're paying attention and interested in what your conversation partner is saying, it's important to maintain eye contact with them throughout the conversation.

- Avoid staring because it can be perceived as aggressive or uneasy.

- Look away from the conversation to avoid staring or making your conversation partner uncomfortable.

- To make your message more engaging and persuasive, use your eyes to convey emotions such as happiness or concern.

Lips

Lips are another important nonverbal cue because they can reveal a lot about our emotions and intentions. Smiling makes you appear more approachable and friendly, whereas frowning makes you appear unfriendly or unapproachable. Consider the following tips to improve your lip use:

- To convey warmth and approachability, use a genuine, natural smile.

- Avoid insincere or manipulative smiles that seem forced or fake.

- Be aware of your voice tone, as it can convey emotions reflected in your lips.

- Use your lips to convey emotions such as happiness or concern to make your message more engaging and persuasive.

Feet

The feet are frequently ignored as a nonverbal cue, but they can reveal a lot about our emotions and intentions. Our feet can indicate whether we're engaged in the conversation or ready to move on. Consider the following suggestions for improving your footwork:

- Face your conversation partner to demonstrate that you're engaged and interested in what they're saying.

- Turning or facing away from your conversation partner can be perceived as rude or disengaged.

- Use your feet to indicate that you're engaged in the conversation, such as by leaning forward slightly or making subtle posture adjustments.

Tap or shuffle your feet to avoid being perceived as distracting or conveying nervousness. Be aware of your overall body language, including your feet, to ensure that your nonverbal cues are consistent and in line with your message.

Unconventional Ways to Improve Your Communication Skills

"C-ca-ca-ca-can I u-u-use the toilet?" I exclaim, unable to contain myself any longer. Giggles can be heard. *"You c-c-ca-can,"* says the instructor. The snickering gets even louder; I turn beet red and rush out.

The bullying I endured after developing a stutter in middle school left me terrified to speak in public. Merely uttering my name caused me to break out in a cold sweat. The psychologist who doubled as my biology professor recommended that I practice pronouncing words aloud in my head before actually saying them.

Speak in Your Mind First

Not expecting it to, but it did the trick. My stammering improved to the point where it wasn't too embarrassing to talk about. I was soon free of it for good, though I still mentally repeated the words long afterward. My communication ability greatly improved as what had been a conscious and deliberate effort turned into an unconscious habit. Some words from a Farnam Street blog:

According to the formula, one must first become consciously incompetent, then consciously competent, and finally become unconsciously competent.

Mind-to-mind communication helps you get your thoughts in order and confirms what you intend to say before you say it. Having said it aloud once will help it make more sense when repeated. In addition, it serves as a "switch" that prevents you from saying foolish things when feeling emotional. Having been a former possessor of a razor's edge, I can attest to the harm that can come from having an unfiltered opinion. Emotional outbursts in conversation can negatively impact how you think and behave in the long run. Since, as science has shown, the subconscious takes everything we say at face value, this is often the case. Shirley Vandersteen, a psychologist, put it this way:

"Not only do your words affect the people and events around you, but they also shape your thoughts and determine your future. Words are a powerful tool for reinforcing and expanding upon your ideas. Your harsh, negative, thoughtless, or judgmental words will draw more

attention to the negative aspects of your experience. You'll soon form the routine of seeing only the negative aspects of everything."

So think the words through first before you utter them. You will be able to convey your thoughts more clearly and accurately, and you will also avoid saying anything that is not what you truly feel. At first, it will be very intentional, but eventually, it will become automatic.

Explain Rocket Science to an 8-Year-Old

He asks, "Why? " while jamming the triangular end of a watermelon slice into the "o" in his mouth. "Exactly what do you mean by "why"? Please stop asking me why "A frustrated says me.

Her gentle brown eyes appear vacant. A deep breath later, I say, "Okay, fine," and go on. "Indeed, as you can see, the process is straightforward. If you have a full address, you would first look up the area or colony, then the street, the building, and finally the apartment number, right?"

I go on as he wildly nods in agreement: "Therefore, it is simple. What if, on the other hand, every structure in the city was numbered instead of having a street, colony, or area name? There's no way you could find the street. That's how the Internet works too."

Oh, yes, now I see it! He exclaims with a sudden ray of optimism. At that point, he tosses the green peel into the trash can and wipes his mouth with the sleeve of his shirt to avoid getting any blood on his young, developing skin.

I heaved a sigh of contentment and relief when it all worked out. Although the kid was bright, he could be a pain to teach. Explaining things to a kid isn't very pleasant, but it's necessary.

One of the most important aspects of good communication is keeping things as simple as possible while still getting your point across. A child is the "simplest" listener you can find; if you can communicate clearly with them, you can communicate clearly with anyone.

Moreover, because few things have such a short attention span as children, you are compelled to keep the talk as interesting as possible: the greatest challenge I faced in my daring mission to enlighten my little cousin about how the Internet works were keeping the child interested.

Think about trying to explain something difficult to a child. It might be a sibling, a nephew, or even someone you've kidnapped. Don't worry; we won't put you in a cell with a bunch of weird inmates and nothing but walls for company.

Tell Yourself to Shut the F*ck Up

Years ago, when I still stuttered, I rarely spoke in public and instead focused on listening to others rather than speaking myself. Though I no longer stuttered, I could still hold decent conversations; in fact, they were markedly superior to those I had after I had become a one-way speaking machine. Ironically, sometimes the best way to improve your communication skills is not to use them. Don't maintain complete silence—that'll scare the other person to death.

However, it does become silent at times. The only way for the other person to speak is to silence yourself first. When the other person joins in, it transforms from a monologue into a conversation.

One of the keys to effective communication is to keep your ears open at all times and switch your mouth on and off at will. The less you say, the better. Most people enjoy expressing themselves and are grateful to those who allow them. The reason is it takes more effort to listen than to speak. Even when I stuttered, I could hold a decent conversation.

We also have two ears and one mouth rather than the reverse. As a result, the next time you have a conversation, every once in a while, tell yourself to shut the f*ck up.

Cringe at Yourself in The Mirror

One of my biggest fears was speaking in front of an audience. And it still is. I used to sweat buckets whenever I held one, but now I can. I used to feel extremely uncomfortable and constantly fidget during conversations, whether one-on-one or in a small group. I do, but only marginally so now.

What shifted was my confidence in how I looked when I spoke in public. The first few times I had to face myself in a mirror and deliver a speech, I got the chills. Everything about my expression, from the smile to the gestures to the way my lips moved, seemed off. That's to be expected, as this was the first time I'd ever seen myself through someone else's eyes.

Mirror practice has been shown to improve self-awareness, body image, and social confidence, according to studies in psychology. Self-compassion is also significantly enhanced by this practice. Get cozy in the mirror, chat with yourself, and shiver uncontrollably. As a result, you'll be more self-aware, confident, and likely to initiate conversation.

To Conclude...

Success correlates directly with one's ability to communicate effectively, as it is the driving force behind all human endeavors. If conventional advice on better expressing yourself does not cut it, then perhaps some alternative methods will. In conclusion,

- Think out what you want to say before you say it. You'll need to try and think about it at first, but eventually, your brain will learn to do this automatically.

- Let's say you must break down a difficult concept for a kid. Keeping him interested and engaged is just as difficult as getting him to grasp the material.

- It's important to remind yourself to be quiet occasionally. Listening is more important than talking when it comes to effective communication.

Chapter 7: How to Improve Communication in Your Relationship

Few people learn constructive methods of communicating in early life. Relational communication is a skill that is honed over time. We learn it from our first family (also known as our "family of origin") and the other relationships we develop. So, treat yourselves with compassion.

Nonetheless, despite being at a loss as to how best to communicate, here are eight ways to mend your couple's communication and get things back on track. Even if it takes many "fits and starts" and constant arguments, couples must find ways to communicate better to overcome the problem, often feeling more frustrated, exhausted, and hopeless. *So, how many of the following do you agree with?*

- It's frustrating and unproductive because our conversations tend to go in circles.

- Sometimes one or both of us will become angry and lash out at the other.

- There is a problem with us being able to listen to each other without interrupting.

- As a result of frustration, we may sometimes withdraw from the conversation.

- It's not uncommon for our friendly chats to escalate into heated arguments.

- We've both tried various methods of communication but to no avail.

- We've fallen into an unhealthy pattern of interaction.

- We can never get past an initial exchange of words before one of us becomes defensive.

- We're feeling trapped and extremely frustrated.

Like a Bad Dance

It's not uncommon for a couple to dance with hardly any stumbles. The two of them can communicate well enough with one another that they can get back on track after an argument or disagreement without damaging their relationship. Good listeners and communicators do more than just show up when someone asks for their attention; they also learn to tune in, express themselves, and respond thoughtfully.

Some people seem to have a natural rhythm and ease when dancing, while others struggle and feel they have two left feet no matter how hard they try. A severe lack of communication marks their relationship. These people's conversations tend to go in circles, covering the same ground repeatedly, leading to frustration and no resolution of the underlying conflict. For instance, when there is a disagreement or conflict, everyone takes on their own role, which only exacerbates the situation. They can't seem to break out of their routine. It can be extremely detrimental to a relationship because it leads to a breakdown in communication.

When one partner is anxious, they may try to increase their physical contact with the other to feel more secure. To calm down, the anxious partner may do the opposite of what their partner needs and create distance. However, many people struggle with effective health communication. When two people have poor communication skills, unhealthy patterns of interaction are likely to develop. The inability to comprehend, name, claim, and articulate one's emotions perpetuates these unhelpful patterns.

Couples develop a "dance" of interactions that is hard to break because the patterns are reinforced over time. Repeated interactions with significant others, such as family members, friends, and coworkers, reinforce these behaviors. It can be challenging for many people, especially couples, to break out of an established routine. What you see is the dance they've choreographed.

The Distancer and the Pursuer

Circular conversations that lead to fights are a common problem in relationships. These are circular conversations in which both parties keep repeating the same points without progressing toward a resolution. It's common for men to withdraw and put distance between themselves and others, while women are more likely to initiate contact. They withdraw because they need space to process the overwhelming emotions they're experiencing.

They might try to get away from everything or distance themselves from the situation. That's because they might prefer to avoid arguments. They possibly need some time and distance to settle down and think clearly. It is not always the case despite being a fundamental distinction between the sexes.

To a greater extent than men, women typically initiate conversation and seek companionship. They may resort to this behavior when their needs are unmet. They are eager to get in touch immediately and work out a solution. Most of the time, they just keep getting worse. The emotional burden has been lifted.

8 Ways to Improve Communication in Your Relationship

1. Ask questions that create deeper conversations

To have more meaningful conversations, try asking more open-ended questions. Don't ask, "Did you have a good day? "; instead, try, "How was your day?" What were the day's most notable events? Is there anything that keeps coming up that you and I can talk about when the time is right?

It entails considering the feelings of others, even if you disagree with them. Everyone can relax and feel secure enough to express their emotions. What's more, this also includes:

- Get things going slowly and steadily. If now is not a good time to talk, when is? It puts both parties on an even keel from the outset of the conversation, and they are more likely to be receptive to one another's feelings and ideas.

- Plan a break in the action. Overdrive mental processing occurs when both people are experiencing intense feelings. Couples can relieve tension and get back to talking about the problem after taking a break for ten, fifteen, or thirty minutes. Make a plan to get back to the discussion later. Keep your feelings in check.

2. Know your communication style

How else would you characterize your style besides the one who initiates contact or withdraws from it? Styles can be

- Passive-aggressive means you are indirectly hostile, sarcastic, devious, untrustworthy, and unable to have productive conversations with others.

- Aggressive people force their wants and needs on others, overreacting, demanding and rude, belligerent and threatening, loud and hostile, and often afraid of others.

  Submissive people avoid taking charge of their own life and struggle to make even the simplest decisions.

- In social and emotional contexts, "assertive people" refer to those who openly express themselves. Individuals are responsible for the outcomes of their own decisions, good or bad.

- Manipulative people are crafty and manipulative in their approach to getting what they want from others.

Here are some questions to ask yourself that will help you better understand your style and gain the insight that can then be used to make positive changes:

- How did you and your first family talk to each other?

- When it comes to interpersonal connections, how have you noticed these recurring patterns?

- Is there a certain way of speaking that you long to but find difficult?

- Why have your previous attempts failed?

3. Learn to recognize negative or bad communication patterns

Similarly to how a dance between two people can become more fluid and natural over time, so can a couple's communication patterns. Inquire if there are any phrases or actions that set off your triggers. Each person's participation helps form and strengthen patterns over time.

The patterns often arise from the unique ways in which people communicate and the unique stresses they experience. How each person reacts to what is being said also reinforces patterns. Consider the origins of these recurring problems, your role in perpetuating them, and the positive changes you'd like to see.

4. Don't expect your partner to read your mind. It never works

Good luck finding a partner who can read your mind if you're the type who keeps things bottled up. We've tried this before, and it never works. To no avail. And the time you spend wondering is not a small cost. It's not weird, I promise.

You must find a way to express your thoughts and feelings to your partner. Telling them what you want from the relationship is part of this. It is a two-way street. You should be as forthright and open as possible when discussing your emotions. Communicate with them as best you can, avoiding blame and using a positive tone and inflection.

5 Try another method of contact

In-person interactions can feel stifling and ill-suited at times. And there are times when texting provides a slight improvement in communication. Texting, for instance, is best reserved for brief, humorous exchanges rather than deep discussions or when you've had a few drinks.

Perhaps a humorous meme you and your friend can relate to would do the trick. Each of us enjoys a good meme. Email may be more convenient for some people (which gives them the time to share feelings). Please use this as a jumping-off point for more in-depth discussions. Some couples start a journal together on their journey to better, more mutually beneficial communication. Put your thinking cap on and discuss what other options might prove more fruitful.

6. Adopt a "WE" mentality

When both partners believe they make a good team, they are more likely to open up to one another and enjoy spending time together. They believe in working together as a team.

They use the pronoun "we" when they need to talk about their emotions. To improve and resolve the conflict, you might say something like, "I wish we could do this better." Constantly using the word "you," laying blame, and pointing fingers will keep you in the same place you are now.

It can also lead to a breakdown in communication and a great deal of resentment in a relationship. And, really, isn't it nicer when nobody's pointing the blame at you?

While you and your partner acknowledge that change is difficult and that you may experience many "fits and starts," it's good to know that you have each other's support as you try to break free of the unhealthy "dance" you've created.

7. Take control of your own feelings

When we're under pressure, our emotions tend to surge. Nothing could be further from the truth. The conversation you want to have with your partner can't be made without first learning how to control your emotions so that you can show up.

Recognizing your emotional and mental triggers can help you better understand yourself. Your spouse or significant other does not owe you an emotional or behavioral change for your convenience. On the other hand, assistance is always available if you need it.

8. Decide on just one subject at a time

Bringing up everything you feel is still unresolved is a surefire way to start a fight. Many couples take advantage of this time to vent their grievances and anger at one another. You should never do that.

As the saying goes, "everything but the kitchen sink" gets thrown in when tempers flare. Everything that's been bothering you, whether it's old wounds or topics that haven't been broached before (but maybe they have, and hey, why not?). It's not hard to picture what's going on here. Bad suggestion. However, it is still done by humans.

A better question would be: what is it? Both parties agree that it is best to set aside specific amounts of time to discuss specific topics. It aids in keeping everyone on track and responsible for their actions.

You'll both improve to the point where you can continue talking, identify your triggers, and figure out how to stay in touch. (It's entirely possible!)

Both parties will feel more confident in their ability to communicate, and the relationship as a whole will strengthen as a result.

There are ways to repair the damage done to your relationship by the negative patterns and poor communication you've established. Starting with a strategy to make manageable adjustments is the first step.

Having a plan reduces the likelihood of tensions rising, leaving both parties feeling hopeless and disoriented. If you want to talk about your plan, the best time to do it is when you and your companion are alone and feeling emotionally and mentally at ease.

The point is to develop a new method of communicating that is both healthier and more effective so that you can continue to learn and adapt to one another over time.

Chapter 8: Effective Communication at Work

Your first official meeting as team leader is in an hour. You've recently been promoted, and it hits you: instead of working with a small team of colleagues, you're now the department head. You're so anxious that your palms are sweating. You looked over the agenda for the meeting several times. Concerned with the thought, "What if they don't like me?" Worst case scenario, they start to have doubts about me. If my message doesn't go through, then what? However, what if I am unable to convey my message?

The ability to communicate effectively is crucial in the business world. If a person has brilliant ideas but cannot articulate them, they are unlikely to be implemented. Conversely, if a person is a gifted communicator but is plagued by terrible ideas, the consequences would be catastrophic. Imagine the number of modern world leaders who have spread false information or stoked fear, causing the deaths of thousands. In light of these instances, it is easy to see how important it is to have open lines of communication.

As a life coach, it has been my mission for over 15 years to facilitate my clients' material, spiritual, and intellectual development. Many highly effective leaders I've observed have surpassed all goals set for them and their teams through the clarity and efficiency of their communication. Many professionals have fallen short in my experience due to poor interpersonal skills; for example, failing to convey their ideas clearly to their teams or clients. However, people vary greatly from one another. How do you choose the most effective method of interaction? One must be aware of and adept at interacting with various communication styles to communicate effectively.

Passive Communicator

Is it common for people you work with or socialize with to say things like, "I don't care," "It's no big deal," or "I just want to keep my cool" when you bring up an issue? If you answered yes, you may be dealing with a passive communicator.

People who are passive communicators are less likely to voice their opinions, feelings, and needs in social situations. They act uninterested, unconcerned, and powerless to reject or oppose what is being presented to them. Passive communicators have the mistaken belief that no one is interested in hearing what they have to say. The inability to communicate externally is a common source of miscommunication, conflict, resentment, and isolation. The inability to easily spot a passive communicator directly results from their tendency to avoid making themselves heard.

Since they don't show it, how can you tell if someone is a passive communicator? A passive communicator can be identified by using the questioning technique. Recognizing those who sit back and observe rather than actively contributing to group discussions is one way to spot a passive communicator. They show this in their communication by not paying attention, not making eye contact, and sitting or standing in the way that seems to object silently that their feelings have not been considered. Passive communicators also tend to be overly modest and quick to apologize. Tracking team members' successes or failures can also reveal the presence of a silent team member. It is not uncommon to see missed deadlines, a lack of enthusiasm for tasks, or even neglect of the assignment from these people because they agree on the surface to avoid conflict but struggle internally. How can you successfully collaborate with passive communicators who shy away from conflict?

Some people are just not talkers, and you will encounter them professionally and personally. You'll have to see the situation from their perspective to communicate effectively with them. You need to reassure them of your interest and appreciation despite their tendency to downplay the significance of their input. You should learn to listen more carefully and avoid interrupting passive communicators to have productive conversations with them. After they have finished speaking, demonstrate your attentiveness by restating what they have said in your own words. They will pick up on the slightest signals of disapproval or disinterest in your tone and body language, so be mindful. It's important to boost their self-assurance by offering positive feedback and reinforcement after they've shared their thoughts and feelings. Finally, it's important to address disagreements head-on and fairly, as passive communicators often repress their feelings, which can be more damaging to a relationship.

Aggressive Communicator

Is there a coworker you know who never stops shouting? Or maybe you have a coworker who tends to get defensive whenever you bring up a sensitive topic? Or consider the managers who seem to have a fixed glare and a harsh tone whenever they address their staff. You have likely just met an aggressive communicator if you know such a person.

Those who use aggressive language are known as aggressive communicators. They enjoy making their points heard with an authoritative voice that demands attention. Some ways they express themselves are through overt displays of hostility, such as making direct eye contact with the audience, walking up to them, making large gestures with their hands, and so on. They resort to name-calling, personal attacks, criticism, or threats to get their point across. Compared to their passive counterparts, aggressive communicators stand out easily and can be difficult to engage with.

There should always be plans to maintain harmony on a team that includes an outspoken communicator. First, you should always remain calm and not let comments bother you. Persons who are aggressive in their communication seek out conflict, as they see it as the only way to convey their message successfully. If you escalate the conflict, your coworkers will likely misinterpret your intentions, forming a negative impression of you. Similarly, the renowned Mexican author Miguel Angel Ruiz once said:

"Keep your emotions in check... To some extent, what others say and do reflect their own internal worldview. Once you've built up immunity to the judgments and actions of others, you won't let them cause you pain."

You can't expect respect and cooperation from an aggressive communicator unless you keep a professional demeanor, establish clear boundaries, and apply appropriate consequences. Communicate assertively and productively at all times to keep the conversation moving forward. Seek out the motivations of these people in a closed-door intervention or meeting if necessary. Keep in mind that composure and adaptability are essential. According to a proverb from ancient China: *"A stone cannot be met with another stone; doing so will destroy both. The stone will sink while the pond will remain calm if you absorb it like water."*

Passive-Aggressive Communicator

Does your company have an office rumormonger? What about a pal who, when sad, often withdraws from social interaction? Or, even better, someone who appears to have "two faces."

Communicators who engage in passive-aggressive behavior appear serene on the surface and use their words to avoid conflict, but their true feelings and dissatisfaction are often revealed in their body language and tone of voice. Unlike passive communicators, passive-aggressive individuals are aware of their own emotions and thoughts. They are self-aware enough to identify the sources of their dissatisfaction, and they often simmer their resentment before expressing it in covert and invisible ways. Recognizing them may be more difficult than other communication styles due to the inherent inconsistency of facial expressions and words.

Passive-aggressive communicators can be identified by their "cold shoulder" or lack of open communication with the other person. Contrary to appearances, they frequently act in opposition to one another. Instead of evaluating their output, you should focus on what they're doing to improve your communication. They would say they would follow you but ultimately do things differently if they disagreed with your methods. Their replies occasionally display a parallel pattern. The passive-aggressive speaker might say, "Okay, I'll do it, but don't be surprised if it doesn't work."

Communicating with passive-aggressive people can be tricky, as they may appear persuasive but disagree. If you're interacting with these types of people, it's important to remember not to take the bait when they try to elicit a reaction from you. Focus on the message rather than the words they used to try to shut you up. Instead of avoiding conflict by avoiding giving direct answers, be confident in the answers you give. Get inside their heads, and don't take criticism personally. Finally, rather than relying on past experiences as a basis for your response, you should always ensure that your response suits the current situation. Those who engage in passive-aggressive communication should always be met with objectivity.

Assertive Communicator

Do you have an amiable pal who can spark a conversation without being too much of a presence? What about a leader who encourages open dialogue and doesn't mind being the subject of criticism? People who can confidently express themselves to others are known as effective communicators.

Communicators who can stand firm in their convictions are universally regarded as the most effective communicators. They are articulate in describing their inner experiences and pleading for empathy from others. Individuals with this trait are receptive to hearing others out and sharing their perspectives and feelings. They are people who constantly talk about themselves or their group. Statements like, "I am worried about the project's progress" or "We are all in this together; let's figure out how to get the project moving forward" are examples. A team's strengths lie in its members, who are its resources, and who are generally a force for good in pursuing the team's objective.

Communicate openly and directly with those people who are confident in themselves. They will foster an environment where people feel comfortable talking to one another and where those conversations are valued. I suggest you take what you can from these people and use open dialogue to reach a common goal. In conversations with confident speakers, you can always feel safe expressing your feelings and needs. Remember that great things occur when a team works together and shares information.

I have devoted the last 15 years of my life to assisting others in achieving success in the three most important areas of life: one's personal life, one's financial life, and one's professional Many of the most successful people I've met in my life have been those whose words carried weight. I've also witnessed many people whose success was stunted by their inability to interact effectively with others. The best way to convey information to another person is never sure because everyone is unique. Determining the most effective means of communication is crucial to achieving one's professional goals. To succeed, you must be familiar with the various communication styles and how to adapt your approach accordingly. *How do you plan to express yourself at the next meeting?*

Chapter 9: Building and Maintaining Relationships

Relationships are an important aspect of our existence. We make friends for various purposes, including companionship, support, and professional networking. Building and maintaining strong relationships is critical for our personal and professional development, and it necessitates the development of a set of skills that can be taught and practiced.

This chapter will examine helpful hints and tactics for establishing and maintaining relationships. We'll talk about how to build rapport, communicate successfully, manage conflict, and sustain long-term relationships, among other things. Whether you want to form new relationships or strengthen existing ones, the strategies in this chapter can help you accomplish your objectives and form strong, long-lasting bonds with others. Strong partnerships have numerous advantages. A trusted network of friends, colleagues, and associates can give emotional support during difficult times, advice and guidance when making important choices, and access to new opportunities and resources. Maintaining strong relationships can lead to new business possibilities, improved job satisfaction, and access to new clients and customers for professionals.

Building and maintaining relationships, on the other hand, is not always simple. It takes time, effort, and excellent communication skills. It can be difficult to find the opportunity to connect with others in today's fast-paced world, and social media and digital communication can sometimes stifle the formation of genuine, meaningful connections.

It is critical to be deliberate about developing and keeping relationships to overcome these obstacles. You can develop a network of trusted friends and colleagues who will support you throughout your life and career by prioritizing relationships and investing the time and effort required to make strong connections with others.

The following parts will look at practical guidelines and strategies for building and maintaining relationships. We'll review subjects like rapport building, efficient communication, conflict resolution, and maintaining long-term relationships. Whether you're an introvert or an extrovert or building personal or professional relationships, the strategies in this chapter can help you accomplish your objectives and form strong, long-lasting bonds with others.

How to Build Sincere Relationships Through Communication

Effective communication is the cornerstone of happy and healthy relationships. When we communicate effectively, we're able to express our feelings and needs in a way that's clear and respectful, and we're able to listen to and understand the perspectives of others. This chapter will explore practical tips and strategies for building happy and healthy relationships through effective communication.

Practice active listening

Active listening is a critical component of effective communication. When we practice active listening, we're fully present and engaged in the conversation, and we're able to understand the perspectives and needs of others. Consider the following tips for practicing active listening:

- Focus on the speaker and avoid distractions.

- Ask clarifying questions to ensure that you understand the speaker's perspective.

- Nodding and making direct eye contact are two great ways to show that you're paying attention and listening.

Use "I" statements

Using "I" statements can help to prevent defensiveness and make the conversation more productive. "I" statements focus on how you feel or perceive the situation rather than assigning blame to the other person. Consider the following example:

- Instead of saying, "You always make me feel frustrated when you're late," say, "I feel frustrated when I have to wait because I'm late for other appointments."

Practice empathy

An empathetic person can identify with and understand the emotions of those around them. Empathy helps us connect with others more meaningfully and strengthens the bonds we share with them. Consider the following tips for practicing empathy:

- Put yourself in the other person's shoes and try to understand their perspective.

- Acknowledge and validate their feelings, even if you don't agree with them.

- Avoid judging or criticizing their feelings or experiences.

Be respectful and avoid criticism

Respectful communication is key to building happy and healthy relationships. Criticism and negative comments can be hurtful and can damage the relationship. Consider the following tips for being respectful:

- Avoid name-calling or other forms of personal attack.

- Focus on the issue, not the person.

- Use a respectful and positive tone of voice.

Practice Assertiveness

Being assertive means articulating your wants and feelings without being aggressive or disrespectful. When we practice assertiveness, we can communicate our needs and boundaries, which helps build healthy relationships. Consider the following tips for practicing assertiveness:

- Use "I" statements to express your needs and feelings.

- Be specific about what you want or need.

- Be respectful and avoid being aggressive or confrontational.

Three Communication Skills for Healthy Relationships

After my coaching call ended, I checked my email and found the message. Twenty minutes before our meeting, my client emailed me to say that he had become ill and asked if we could reschedule. I hadn't read his email, and during our "Hi, how are you?" greeting, he hadn't mentioned needing to reschedule. The usual depth and intimacy of our sessions seemed to be lacking.

Later, when I saw his email, I was disappointed. I thought back on the times I tried to be adaptable or get the job done without asking for what I needed.

When I was younger, I mistakenly believed that demanding my needs be met was the same as being self-centered. My experience has taught me the value of being direct about my wants and needs, particularly in close relationships. The word "ask" stands out in that sentence.

First word: ask

To request is to "ask." Responses to requests can be yes, no, or a request for further discussion. Sharing your needs with others lets them help you get what you want. What if they find you too dependent or unworthy of their affection? It is a possibility. But what if you rush in without the resources you need? It will lead to subpar results and potential negative evaluations of your competence. Other people won't judge you; instead, they may admire your confidence or relief that you've shared your viewpoint.

It's important to keep in mind that asking is different from demanding. There is only one possible response to demand. The demands of others can provoke anger in those who aren't used to dealing with them. To illustrate, let's pretend you and your partner have asked to delay your vacation by two weeks so that you can deal with a crisis at work. He cannot provide the assistance you require at this time or chooses not to. After making the request, it's up to you to accept the result with good grace and make the most of the situation. Possible time or place adjustments could be made. However, this might not always be the case. If that's the case, you'll have to keep looking until you find a solution that works for you. Keeping that in mind may be challenging.

The ask word, right there. You shouldn't expect always to get your way just because you ask for what you want.

Second word: Need

You know the Rolling Stones' song "You Can't Always Get What You Want," right? Aiming for the moon by demanding everything we want could backfire. I can think of many things I want, including more cash, a trimmer physique, and abundant sunshine. Shorter now is the list of things we need. It's essential to our survival and daily functioning; without it, we won't get far.

As a recently divorced mother, I realized I needed regular alone time. I would become so brittle and annoying in its absence that nobody would want to be near me. I included his request for it in my co-parenting plan with him after we divorced. It was a place to relax and not worry about the kids or the job on Sundays. (Saturdays were my husband's free time.) In retrospect, I can see how helpful those hours were in helping me get my bearings and refuel for the week ahead. Every parent has different needs for peace. For some, this may be just a "want" or doesn't make the cut. As far as I was concerned, it was a necessity.

Learning to differentiate between wants and needs is crucial. The ability to express our wants and needs is greatly enhanced. When we know what we need exactly, it's easier to keep going when the first person we ask says no.

And if we don't inquire, then what? To the best of our ability, we press on. Nonetheless, our success cannot be sustained forever. People who count on us—whether family members, romantic partners, close friends, or coworkers—will be let down by our lackluster performance.

There will be a gradual depletion of momentum, energy, and enthusiasm until we survive daily until the candle goes out.

In my experience, those who are the most giving and caring have the hardest time asking for what they need. Because it's a skill, you can learn it.

Finding the Words to Express Your Desires

Needs must be determined as a first step. What am I hoping to gain from this partnership? Decipher your needs from your wants. Do I have sufficient support? To that end, may I inquire about the nature of my request? Need some space, appreciation, help, or fresh opportunities?

Try asking people around you for things and seeing how they respond. It's best to take baby steps at first.

Carefully consider both the content and format of your inquiry. It's important to think about your tone of voice and rehearse the words you'll use before making a difficult request. Being hostile will not get you anywhere while remaining neutral or cordial will.

Take note of the reactions you receive. To get a "yes" is a simple matter. Saying "no" or "renegotiate" is more difficult skillfully. Learn to accept the answer "no" with grace. Put some space between phrases. You could try paraphrasing it to give yourself time to process what the other person just said. To which she replied, "So you're saying you can't do this for these reasons..." If you find yourself at a loss for words, simply saying, "I need to think about this; let's revisit tomorrow," will leave the conversation open.

Third word: Offer

We have examined two words: need and ask.

An offer is the third term. Likewise important is our readiness to assist others in obtaining their goals. Discord and resentment can creep into our relationships if this is lacking.

Giving something to another person, whether it be help, time, or money, requires us to be selfless. The spirit of giving aids in the development of relationships. Also necessary is paying close attention to the well-being of our loved ones. It's great to ask if you need anything, but it's also very encouraging to say something like, "You look like you could use a hug, is that right?" alternatively, "Would calling a plumber help?"

When we offer something to someone, we are not only expressing our generosity but also giving them the option to take what we offer. Don't assume they want or need what we're offering them, and don't count on them to accept it. It's up to them to make the call. It can be challenging when we are confident that our suggestion will benefit them. Once again, drills are in order. Rehearse making offers without worrying about what people will say. The triad of words "ask," "need," and "offer" sums it all up. At the moment, which one do you employ the most effectively? What's the most challenging? How will improving your skill at using it affect your relationships?

Maintaining Relationships Through Digital Communication

Maintaining relationships through digital communication has become increasingly important in today's digital age. With so many people working remotely and connecting through social media and email, it's more important than ever to have effective strategies for staying connected with others. In this chapter, we'll explore practical tips and strategies for maintaining relationships through digital communication, including examples of messages or emails to send.

Schedule regular check-ins

One of the most important things you can do to maintain relationships through digital communication is to schedule regular check-ins with your contacts. It could be a weekly or monthly check-in, depending on the nature of your relationship. During these check-ins, you can share updates, ask how the other person is doing, and stay connected. Here's an example of a message you might send to schedule a check-in:

"Hi [name], I hope you're doing well! I wanted to see if you're available for a quick catch-up next week. How does [date and time] work for you?"

Share interesting content

Sharing interesting content is a great way to stay connected with others and maintain relationships. This could be an article, a video, a podcast, or something else you think your contact would find interesting. Here's an example of an email you might send to share interesting content:

"Hi [name], I found this article today and thought you might find it interesting. It's about [topic] and has some great insights. Let me know what you think!"

Show gratitude

Expressing gratitude is important to maintaining relationships, and digital communication is convenient. Whether you're thanking someone for their support or expressing appreciation for something they've done, taking the time to show gratitude can go a long way in building and maintaining relationships. Here's an example of an email you might send to express gratitude:

"Hi [name], I just wanted to take a moment to say thank you for all of your help with [project/task]. Your support has been invaluable, and I'm grateful to have you on my team."

Offer help or support

Offering help or support is another great way to maintain relationships through digital communication. Whether you're offering to provide advice, make an introduction, or help with a project, showing that you're willing to lend a hand can help to strengthen your relationships with others. Here's an example of an email you might send to offer help or support:

"Hi [name], I heard that you're working on [project/task], and I wanted to offer my support. If there's anything I can do to help, whether providing advice or lending a hand, please don't hesitate to reach out. I'm here to help!"

Celebrate milestones

Finally, celebrating milestones is a great way to maintain relationships through digital communication. Whether it's a birthday, a work anniversary, or a personal accomplishment, taking the time to acknowledge and celebrate these milestones can help to strengthen your relationships with others. Here's an example of an email you might send to celebrate a milestone:

"Hi [name], I heard that it's your work anniversary this week, and I wanted to take a moment to say congratulations! It's been great working with you over the past [period], and I'm looking forward to many more successful years together. Keep up the great work!"

Maintaining relationships through digital communication is important to building and maintaining strong connections with others. By scheduling regular check-ins, sharing interesting content, showing gratitude, offering help or support, and celebrating milestones, you can stay connected with others and build lasting relationships. Whether you're connecting with colleagues, friends, or family members, these strategies can help you stay connected and maintain strong relationships in today's digital world. Remember to be genuine, authentic, and thoughtful in your digital communications and to respect the other person's time and boundaries.

CONCLUSION

In this book, we've looked at various practical strategies and guidelines for speaking confidently to anyone. We've covered everything from rapport development and active listening to anxiety management and communication barriers. By implementing these strategies, you can become a more confident and effective communicator and create powerful, long-lasting connections with others.

The ability to connect with others, comprehend their perspectives, and convey your own ideas and emotions clearly and compellingly is at the heart of successful communication. You can develop the skills needed to do so and the confidence needed to communicate effectively in any circumstance by using the methods in this book. Remember that successful communication includes both speaking and listening. You can strengthen relationships and create a more positive, collaborative atmosphere by actively listening to others and being open to new ideas and viewpoints.

Finally, successful communication is about being genuine, authentic, and empathetic. By putting yourself in the other person's shoes and approaching communication with an open mind and heart, you can create a more positive and productive discussion that helps all parties involved.

So, whether you're an introvert or an extrovert, talking with coworkers, friends, or family members, the techniques in this book can help you become a more confident and effective communicator. By implementing these strategies and continuing to learn and grow as a communicator, you can become more effective and influential and create the relationships and connections that will help you achieve your personal and professional objectives.